# Japanese Style Companion Planting

## Organic Gardening Techniques for Optimal Growth and Flavor

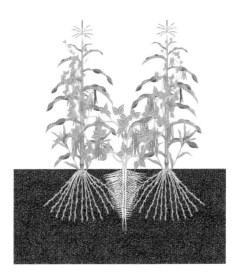

Toshio Kijima

**TUTTLE** Publishing

Tokyo | Rutland, Vermont | Singapore

# CONTENTS

## Grow Delicious Fruit: Companion Plants for Fruits

## Column

✳ Cropping seasons use Kanto Area (Japan) as reference.

# Choosing Companion Plants to Grow Delicious Vegetables

### A Symbiotic Relationship

"Companion planting" is a cultivation technique that is crucial to growing healthy and delicious vegetables without relying on pesticide or chemical fertilizer.

Many plants naturally compete against each other within the limited space available in order to receive the most benefits. However, it is rare for a plant to completely dominate a given space—plants find a way to coexist, splitting spaces via root depth, height and other factors.

There are many advantages to different types of plants growing together. First, plants gathering together can avoid rain and wind and prevent soil erosion. Second, cultivating different plants diversifies the environment and can minimize disease and pest damage. Third, plants create a network of nutrients through their bacterial thread to enhance each other's growth.

Although it seems that plants tend to compete against each other to survive, plants can coexist and even develop a win-win relationship by having a positive influence on each other.

### Companion plants: Experience and knowledge put together

It has long been known that these phenomena occur, and this knowledge has been applied to farming for ages, especially on Asian farms where space is often limited.

Nowadays, mixed cultivation of scallions with cucumber or pumpkin is widely practiced around the globe. This was originally inspired by traditional farming techniques in which farmers in the Tochigi Prefecture prevented repeated cultivation damage by planting scallions with white-flowered gourd, a Liliaceae plant. When this method was studied scientifically, it

was discovered that scallions have rhizosphere microorganisms that release bactericidal agents. Upon further investigation, it was discovered that other Alliaceae plants also have the same microorganisms, and that you could apply the same knowledge to different plant combinations. For example, tomatoes or eggplants work well with garlic chives, while strawberries work well with scallions.

Although there are many plant pairings like the ones discussed in this book, few have had scientific explanations as to why they make good combinations. You could say that companion planting is a result of many years of experience and knowledge put together. If each combination has clear benefits, and those benefits can be recreated in different places and at different times, then there's no reason not to apply this knowledge to your own food gardening! Let's grow healthy and delicious vegetables in confined spaces by making the best use of the plants' nature and innate power.

—Toshio Kijima

 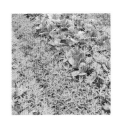  

# What is Companion Planting? The Four Benefits

 ## Prevents Disease

### Get rid of antagonistic bacteria using the power of microorganisms

Alliaceae plants such as scallions and garlic chives have microorganisms on the roots that release an antibiotic substance that can reduce the risk of diseases for Cucurbitaceae/Solanaceae plants.

Example: Cucumber x Scallions, Tomato x Garlic chives, Strawberry x Garlic, etc.

### Use mycoparasites to prevent diseases

Plants such as barley and oats commonly suffer from powdery mildew. Certain plants increase the number of mycoparasites that are attracted to the mildew bacteria.

Example: Cucumber x Wheat, Grape x Oat, etc.

 ## Repels pests

### Get rid of pests using scents and colors

Plants develop a defense mechanism in order to avoid being prey to insects. Through stages of evolution, some insects gained the ability to neutralize toxins—these are the insects we call pests. However, pests are tolerant only of the toxins from certain kinds of plants. They determine whether a plant is dangerous to them by the plant's smell or its color. You can confuse insects when you grow different types of plants together.

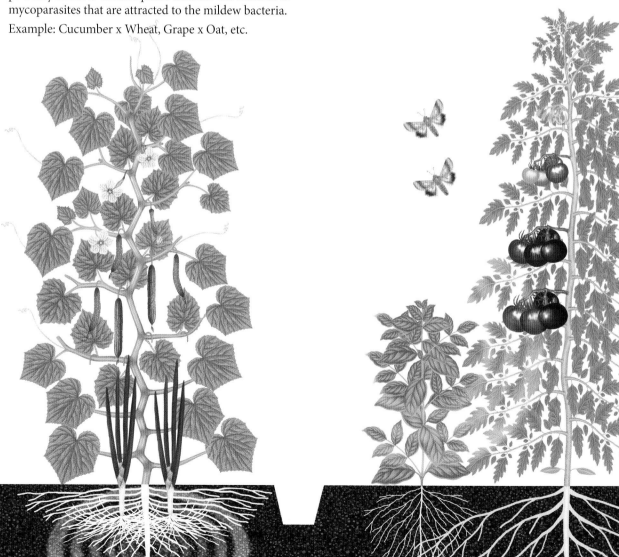

*Companion plants are the plants that grow well when planted in close proximity to each other. In Japanese, the word can be literally translated to "Mutual prosperity plants"; however, while there are plants that are mutually beneficial, there are some combinations in which one plant serves the other, but receives no benefits. The benefits of companion plants can be sorted into four categories. There are plant combinations that fit in multiple categories.*

## Increase the number of natural enemies

While pests are attracted to only certain types of plants, their enemies (also called beneficial insects) tend to eat a wide variety of pests. "Banker plants" take advantage of this phenomenon—you can reduce the number of pests on vegetables by cultivating another type of plant that can attract beneficial insects.

## Speeds up growth
### Get positive results from giving your plants an appropriate level of stress

When different types of vegetables are grown near each other, plants grow taller than usual, or you can increase the size of the harvest. The roots of each plant enhance the other's growth, making it easier for roots to absorb water and air. It is also suggested that the substance released from the leaves, stems and roots, or the microorganisms on the roots, induce better absorption of nutrients. As companion planting gives an appropriate level of stress to the plants, they sometimes grow more flowers or become stronger against climate change or pests. Also, Fabaceae plants have microorganisms that can enrich the soil and enhance another plant's growth.

## Efficient use of space
### Grow more than one plant in the same space

Efficient use of space is one of the biggest advantages of companion planting. If the plants can grow well together, you can grow them in the same space. This follows an old Japanese principle that you can only fit so many walnuts in a bowl, but the spaces between the walnuts can hold grains of millet. You can grow another type of plant using bits of open space in a planter or bed. This is especially useful for farming in a place with limited space, like a kitchen garden.

# Maximize the Benefits!
# Basics and Tips for Cultivation

## Mixed Planting
Grow different vegetables on one furrow

### THE BASICS
Grow another type of vegetable in-between your vegetable seedlings. The principle is that the original plant has about the same size of harvest as when it is planted on its own, while the companion could potentially have a larger than usual harvest, increasing the overall harvest. The key components are the positioning of the plants and the timing of starting cultivation.

### TIPS
Make the best of your vegetable garden by knowing and understanding different plants' characteristics. For example, the combination of tomatoes x peanuts pairs a tall plant and short plant; at the same time, it pairs a nutrient-absorbing plant with nutrient-releasing plant. As peanuts love a lot of sunlight, it is better to grow them on the edge of the furrow instead of between the tomato seedlings. Peanuts also act as mulch by covering the ground with their leaves and stems.

    The pairing of a Brassicaceae plant (cabbage) with an Asteraceae plant (green leaf lettuce) is primarily to avoid pest damage on the cabbage. Usually, it's sufficient to have one green leaf lettuce seedling per 4–5 cabbage seedlings; but you can increase the number of green leaf lettuce seedlings if the cabbage is dealing with a lot of damage from pests.

## Intercropping
Utilize plants' differing growing periods

### THE BASICS
Intercropping is the practice of growing plants with overlapping cultivation periods. Although companions are usually cultivated during the same period, this takes advantage of long and short cultivation periods of compatible plants. For example, as eggplants have a long cultivation period between spring and fall, in spring, you can grow vineless green beans, and after the summer you can grow daikon.

### TIPS
In the combination of spring-harvested cabbage and fava beans, cabbage acts as a shield against wind to protect fava beans. It is important to consider the wind direction in this case; simply planting them together will not work.

    The purpose of planting crimson clover on the onion patch is to enrich the soil. The purpose of planting celery between taro seedlings is to give shade to the celery seedlings. It's important have a concrete understanding of why you are pairing one plant with another.

    Potatoes and taro pair up well because you can start growing taro before harvesting potatoes. Taro is planted on the lower ground under earthed-up potatoes, making it easier to earth up taro later. Always consider efficiency when choosing combinations.

## Some Basic Patterns in Mixed Planting and Intercropping

**Monocotyledonous plant x dicotyledonous**
Mixed planting of green pepper (dicotyledonous) and garlic chives (monocotyledonous). These types have different types of mycorrhizal microorganisms and require different types of nutrients to grow.

**Deep-rooted plants x shallow-rooted plants**
Mixed planting of spinach (deep-rooted) and green onion (shallow rooted). The roots do not compete against one another.

**Tall plant x short plant**
Peanuts (short plant) grows well on the foot of eggplants (tall plant). As the leaf growth of these plants is mutually non-interfering, you can benefit from the efficient use of space.

*In order to maximize the benefits of companion plants, you need to manage the cultivation period, distance between plants, and plant species. Through gaining experience, you can find your own way of using companion plants. Here, we will explain the basics and tips of companion plant cultivation by splitting the method into three patterns.*

## Relay Planting

Plant compatible plants one after the other

### THE BASICS

Companion plants that work well when they are planted together at the same time can also work if they are planted one after the other. As the cultivation of the first plant can create an ideal environment for the second plant, you can benefit not only from the enhanced growth of the second plant but also from the efficiency of cultivation.

### TIPS

You can reduce antagonistic bacteria and prevent diseases depending on the combination. For example, you can plant onions and then pumpkin or fall eggplants. Another example is to plant cabbage after daikon.

You can reduce the amount of fertilizer needed if you use soil enriched by the cultivation of edamame. However, Chinese cabbage requires more fertilizer than, say, broccoli if planted after edamame. It is best to know and understand the characteristics and after-effects of the plants you are growing.

### ◎ Combinations you should avoid

There are plant combinations that have an adverse effect on each other—the opposite of companion plants. For example, when you grow potatoes near cabbage, the cabbage's allelopathy slows down the potatoes' growth. In the photo below, you can see that the row of potatoes that was planted right next to the cabbage row is smaller.

There are also combinations that have the same common pests and diseases. While cucumber and green beans help each other's growth, they both suffer from root-knot nematode. Therefore, avoid this combination if your garden frequently struggles with this microscopic parasite. See p. 127 for combinations you should avoid.

**Sunlight-loving plant x plant that grows well in shade**
Ginger grows underneath the taro leaves. You can not only use the space efficiently, but you can also improve the quality of harvest.

**Nutrient absorbing plant x soil enriching plant**
Corn absorbs a lot of nutrients from a wide area of soil. Edamame and corn, which are both Fabaceae plants, enrich the soil with their root nodule bacteria.

**Long cultivation period x short cultivation period**
You can harvest arugula using the space on the furrow before daikon grows bigger. You can benefit from the pest-repelling scent of arugula as well.

# Companion Plants That Work Together

## Mixed Planting, Intercropping

Here we will introduce examples of combinations suitable for
companion planting, a method by which multiple crops are
planted together during the same season; and intercropping,
a method by which crops' planting seasons overlap. Not only
vegetables but also herbs, flowers and weeds are paired up using
these methods.

# Tomatoes & Peanuts

Speeds up growth   Efficient use of space

## Improvement in tomatoes' growth and useful mulch growth

Tomatoes often struggle to bear fruit when they are overfertilized, and the fruit they do bear can be watery. When you pair them with peanuts, the root nodule bacteria on the peanuts' roots capture the nitrogen in the atmosphere and provide the tomatoes with healthy mineral nutrients.

Peanuts' roots cover the ground like mulch, and help the soil retain moisture. Excess water will be absorbed by the peanut plant, so the humidity level of the ground will be stable. This results in the growth of sweet, high quality tomatoes and a lower incidence of cracked fruit.

**Application** Mixed planting with peanuts can also apply to eggplants and green peppers.

## CULTIVATION PROCESS

**Selecting varieties** Any common varieties will work.

**Mixing soil** If the soil works well for other plants, there is no need to add manure. If the soil is poor, prepare the soil by adding fully matured compost and fermented organic fertilizer three weeks before planting. When growing peanuts, it's important to consider the climate. While peanuts can grow in cooler climates, the soil may have particular needs.

**Planting** Plant both tomatoes and peanuts between late April to late May.

**Sprout nipping for tomatoes** It is recommended to remove the auxiliary sprouts and grow only one sprout.

**Adding fertilizer** Not necessary.

**Harvesting** Harvest tomatoes as soon as they are ripe. You can harvest the fruits until grounds start getting frosty. Peanuts can be harvested when their leaves start to yellow, which can be right around the time of the first frost.

## TIP

Once peanut plants have reached 6–10" (15–20 cm), earth up around the plants to encourage pod growth.

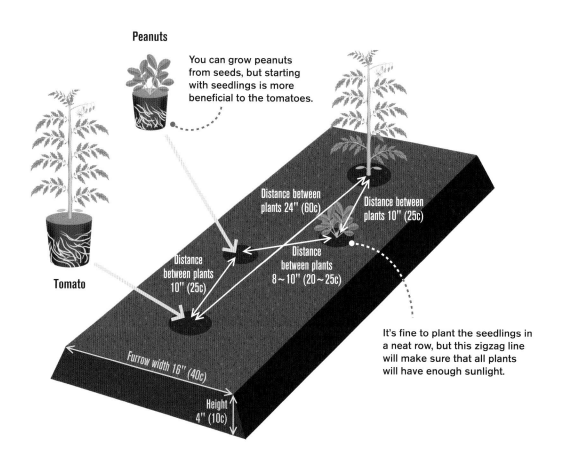

**Peanuts**

You can grow peanuts from seeds, but starting with seedlings is more beneficial to the tomatoes.

**Tomato**

Distance between plants 24" (60c)

Distance between plants 10" (25c)

Distance between plants 10" (25c)

Distance between plants 8~10" (20~25c)

It's fine to plant the seedlings in a neat row, but this zigzag line will make sure that all plants will have enough sunlight.

Furrow width 16" (40c)

Height 4" (10c)

# Let's look at the effects

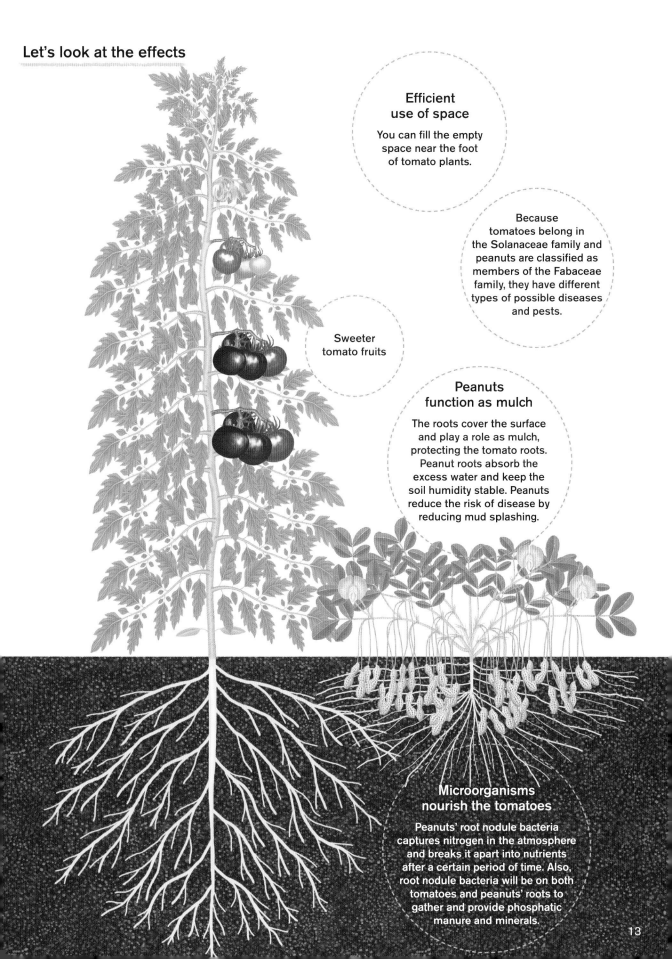

**Efficient use of space**

You can fill the empty space near the foot of tomato plants.

Because tomatoes belong in the Solanaceae family and peanuts are classified as members of the Fabaceae family, they have different types of possible diseases and pests.

Sweeter tomato fruits

**Peanuts function as mulch**

The roots cover the surface and play a role as mulch, protecting the tomato roots. Peanut roots absorb the excess water and keep the soil humidity stable. Peanuts reduce the risk of disease by reducing mud splashing.

**Microorganisms nourish the tomatoes**

Peanuts' root nodule bacteria captures nitrogen in the atmosphere and breaks it apart into nutrients after a certain period of time. Also, root nodule bacteria will be on both tomatoes and peanuts' roots to gather and provide phosphatic manure and minerals.

# Tomatoes & Basil

Speeds up growth    Repels pests

## The scent of basil functions as pest repellent. Also sweetens the fruit

While both basil and tomato plants have allelopathic (influences other plants by releasing biochemicals) potential, these two also have great chemistry. Basil's refreshing scent will repel plant lice (aphids) from the tomato plant. The distance between basil and tomatoes is the key: if they're too close, the resulting shade will prevent basil from growing; if they're too far apart, the pest repellent effect is weakened.

Even if the weather is rainy for multiple days in a row, basil moderately absorbs water, so tomato fruits will not become too watery, but will be sweet.

## CULTIVATION PROCESS

**Selecting varieties** As for tomatoes, any common variety will work. For basil, "Sweet Basil," purple "Dark Opal Basil" and "Purple Ruffle Basil" are good choices. Before planting, prepare seedlings by planting seeds a month prior.

**Mixing soil** If the soil works well for other plants, there is no need to add manure. If the soil is poor, prepare the soil by adding fully matured compost and fermented organic fertilizer three weeks before planting.

**Planting** Plant both tomatoes and basil between late April to late May.

**Sprout nipping for tomatoes** It is recommended to remove the auxiliary sprouts and grow only one sprout.

**Adding fertilizer** Not necessary.

**Harvesting** For tomatoes, harvest the fruits as soon as they are ripe. You can harvest the fruits until the ground starts getting frosty.

## TIP

Once basil grows 5–6 pairs of leaves, cut the middle stem and harvest the top two pairs. Auxiliary sprouts should be pinched out as they come out. This softens the leaves and strengthens the scent, making the pest repellent properties more effective. If you wish to stop growing tomatoes and want to start cultivating a new plant, you can cut the plant short and replant the lower half. Then, basil will grow until the end of fall and can be harvested.

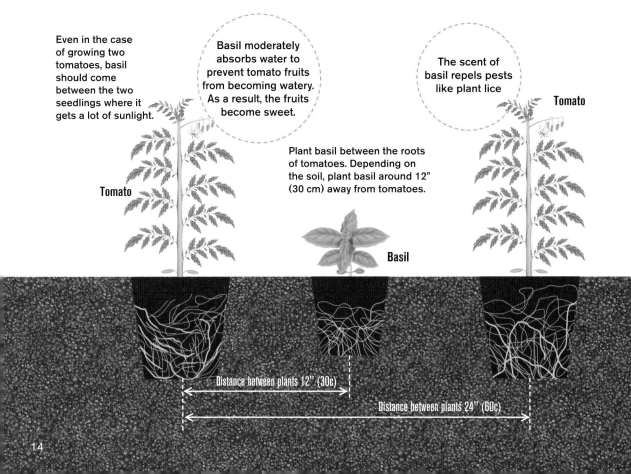

Even in the case of growing two tomatoes, basil should come between the two seedlings where it gets a lot of sunlight.

Basil moderately absorbs water to prevent tomato fruits from becoming watery. As a result, the fruits become sweet.

The scent of basil repels pests like plant lice

Tomato

Plant basil between the roots of tomatoes. Depending on the soil, plant basil around 12" (30 cm) away from tomatoes.

Tomato

Basil

Distance between plants 12" (30c)

Distance between plants 24" (60c)

# Tomatoes & Garlic Chives

## Microorganisms on the garlic chive roots decrease the amount of pathogenic bacteria in soil

Alliaceae family plants such as garlic chives and leek have antagonistic bacteria that produce an antibiotic compound cohabiting on the surface of the roots, decreasing the amount of pathogenic bacteria in the soil that cause wilt disease, a common problem for tomatoes.

Rather than green onions that have shallow roots, garlic chives that have roots as deep as tomatoes work best. Plant three garlic chive plants on each side of one tomato plant. The trick is to plant the pairs close enough to each other that their roots will almost touch. Above the ground, the scent of garlic chives is good pest control.

**Application** Mixed planting of garlic chives also applies to other Solanaceae plants such as eggplants and green peppers (see p. 23).

### CULTIVATION PROCESS

**Selecting varieties** Any common tomato variety will work. Plant garlic chive seeds in pots early March. Because garlic chive seedlings won't be big enough when it's time to plant the tomatoes, it is safer to plant seeds between mid-September and mid-October in the previous year, or to buy seedlings.

**Mixing soil** If the soil successfully grows other plants, there is no need for initial manure. If the soil is poor, prepare the soil by adding fully matured compost and fermented organic fertilizer three weeks before planting

**Planting** Plant both tomatoes and garlic chives between late April to late May.

**Sprout nipping for tomatoes** It is recommended to remove the auxiliary sprouts and grow only one sprout.

**Adding fertilizer** Not necessary.

**Harvesting** For tomatoes, harvest the fruits as soon as they are ripe. You can harvest the fruits until ground starts getting frosty.

### TIP

Continue increasing the number of leaves and tillers. Once the leaves have grown tall, leave 1–1½" (2–3 cm) of the garlic chives above the ground and harvest. By harvesting frequently, garlic chives will keep growing soft leaves and releasing strong scents. Once the harvesting season for tomatoes is over, replant the garlic chives elsewhere so they can be used the following year.

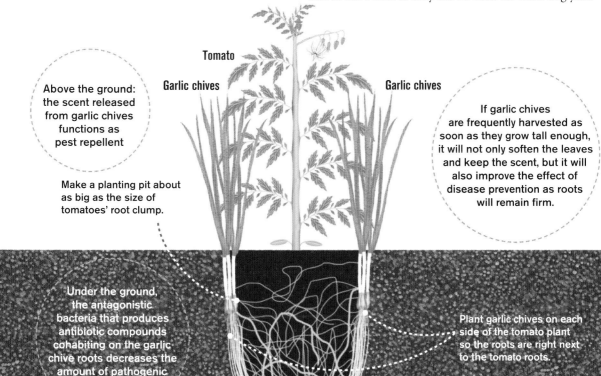

Tomato

Garlic chives

Garlic chives

Above the ground: the scent released from garlic chives functions as pest repellent

If garlic chives are frequently harvested as soon as they grow tall enough, it will not only soften the leaves and keep the scent, but it will also improve the effect of disease prevention as roots will remain firm.

Make a planting pit about as big as the size of tomatoes' root clump.

Under the ground, the antagonistic bacteria that produces antibiotic compounds cohabiting on the garlic chive roots decreases the amount of pathogenic bacteria.

Plant garlic chives on each side of the tomato plant so the roots are right next to the tomato roots.

# Eggplants & Ginger

Speeds up growth

Repels pests

Efficient use of space

## Improve the size of the harvest by using the shade made by the eggplants

Eggplants, from May (when they are planted) to November (when they are put away), take up the space in the furrow. As they become taller, there is more space available near the roots, so let's grow other plants by using this space!

Ginger's cultivation period is almost the same as eggplant's. What is even better is that ginger also grows well in the shade. Therefore, plant ginger where the eggplant leaves create shade. Eggplants grow deep roots that absorb water from the soil beneath them. This makes it easier for ginger, which enjoys having a lot of water, to absorb water as well. Ginger and eggplants seek different nutrients from the soil, so they will not complete, but will instead improve each other's size or harvest.

### CULTIVATION PROCESS

**Selecting varieties** Any variety will work for both eggplant and ginger. However, eggplant will grow stronger if it is a grafted seedling.

**Mixing soil** Three weeks before planting, add fully matured compost and fermented organic fertilizer to prepare.

**Planting** Plant both eggplants and ginger around late April to late May. Split the ginger into pieces, about 1¾ ounce (50 g) apiece. Plant three ginger pieces in a line, at points where eggplants would create shade.

**Adding fertilizer** For eggplants, add a handful of fermented organic fertilizer twice a month on the surface of the furrow.

**Straw mulching** Both eggplants and ginger hate being dehydrated. Put down a layer of straw to serve as mulch.

**Harvesting** Harvest eggplant fruits as they mature. Harvest ginger and eggplants simultaneously in November before the ground gets frosty.

### TIP

Ginger does not like strong sun during mid-summer. It is also fine to harvest ginger during the latter half of summer as leaf ginger, when you do the root cutting for the eggplants.

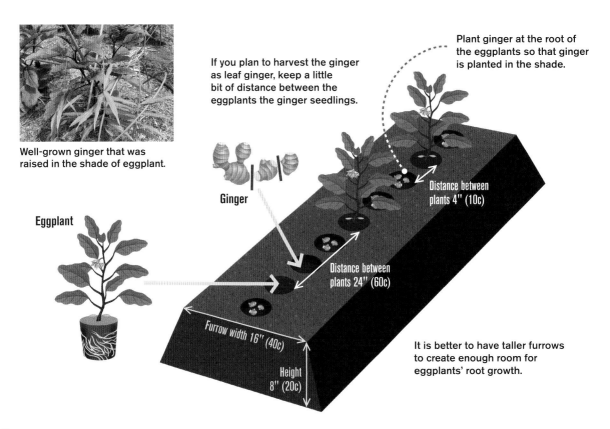

Well-grown ginger that was raised in the shade of eggplant.

If you plan to harvest the ginger as leaf ginger, keep a little bit of distance between the eggplants the ginger seedlings.

Plant ginger at the root of the eggplants so that ginger is planted in the shade.

Distance between plants 4" (10c)

Ginger

Eggplant

Distance between plants 24" (60c)

Furrow width 16" (40c)

Height 8" (20c)

It is better to have taller furrows to create enough room for eggplants' root growth.

# Let's look at the effects

## Repels pests

Ginger tends to have Asian corn worm moths and eggplants often have adzuki bean worms. When the plants are paired, it becomes rarer for moths to fly and lay eggs on the plants, preventing any future damage caused by these pests.

## Acts as a sunshade in mid-summer

Ginger cannot handle strong sun in the summer. Eggplants' leaves create just the right amount of shade.

Straw serves as mulch and keeps the soil moist.

## Prevents diseases

Ginger's bactericide effects decrease the amount of antagonistic bacteria in the soil.

## Easier to keep the soil moist

Eggplants grow deep roots, whereas ginger grows shallow ones. Eggplant roots absorb the water from the deeper layer of soil to make it easier for ginger roots to absorb water.

## Prevents fertilizer overload

Organic substances are broken into ammonia nitrogen and later become nitrate nitrogen. As ginger uses ammonia nitrogen and eggplants use nitrate nitrogen, an overload of nitrate nitrogen can be prevented.

# Eggplants & Vineless Green Beans

 Speeds up growth  Efficient use of space   Repels pests

## Enrich the soil by mixing Fabaceae plants and protect the base from dehydration

Vineless green beans, a Fabaceae family plant, have root nodule bacteria and capture the nitrogen in the atmosphere. Here, the nitrogen will primarily help grow the beans, but some of it will enrich the near-by soil as it separates from the root nodule or is released from the root as waste. Therefore, companion planting of vineless green beans will enhance the growth of eggplants. Also, vineless green beans are short in height and grow densely to create shade near the eggplant roots. This keeps the soil moist. As eggplants and vineless green beans are from different plant families, plant lice and spider mites on eggplants will avoid the beans, and vice versa, reducing damage from pests.

**Application** Instead of vineless green beans, you can also use peanuts (see p. 12). You can also obtain similar effects when you plant green beans with peanuts.

## CULTIVATION PROCESS

**Selecting varieties** For green beans, choose a vineless variety. As for eggplants, a grafted seedling will yield a stronger plant.

**Mixing soil** Three weeks before planting, add fully matured compost and fermented organic fertilizer to prepare.

**Planting, seeding** Plant the eggplants late April to late May. Plant the bean seeds either at the same time or a little later.

**Thinning** Pluck out the leaf that grows after a cotyledon to keep the plant's single-dual base.

**Adding fertilizer** For eggplants, add a handful of fermented organic fertilizer twice a month on the surface of the furrow. If you add too much, the beans will grow too many leaves and too few flowers.

**Harvesting** Harvest eggplant fruits as they mature. The harvesting period for the beans will begin at around 60 days after planting seeds and will last about 10 days. Instead of plucking the plants, cut them at the base.

**Straw mulching** Once you clear away the beans, immediately place straw to use as mulch.

### TIP

Harvest your beans early, when they are a little premature. If you harvest them too late, they will not only be tough and tasteless, but they will also prevent eggplants from growing. You can keep the leaves and stems that you cut at the base to use as mulch. You can also replant them and harvest them in fall.

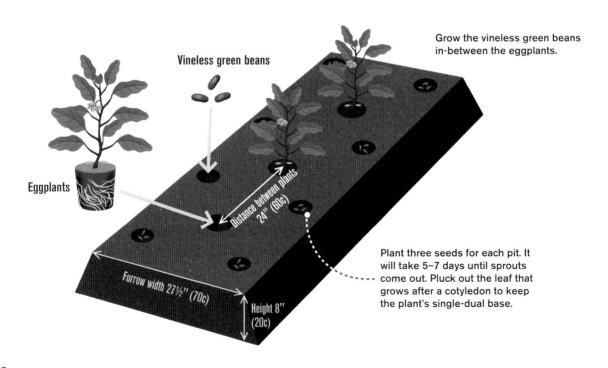

Vineless green beans

Eggplants

Grow the vineless green beans in-between the eggplants.

Distance between plants 24" (60c)

Furrow width 27½" (70c)

Height 8" (20c)

Plant three seeds for each pit. It will take 5–7 days until sprouts come out. Pluck out the leaf that grows after a cotyledon to keep the plant's single-dual base.

# Eggplants & Daikon Radishes

Efficient use of space   Speeds up growth

## Grow and harvest daikon in the fall using the empty space at the foot of the eggplant plants

By around mid-summer, eggplants will have grown tall and have deep roots. They will also be able to withstand a little bit of dehydration. You can use the space near the base to grow daikon.

In early August, plant the daikon seeds after you prune the stems and cut the roots of eggplants. Daikon plants enjoy the shade created by the eggplant leaves and are more likely to sprout, as they are protected from strong summer sun. If daikon seeds are planted around this time, you can harvest them in around 60–80 days.

**Application** Instead of daikon, you can also plant cabbage, Santou-na cabbage or Chinese cabbage early. You can grow green leaf lettuce in the summer—these usually don't fare well during the summer, but can grow well in the shade created by the eggplant leaves.

### CULTIVATION PROCESS

**Selecting varieties** For both eggplants and daikon, any variety will work. However, some daikon varieties are better than others for planting from seeds.

**Mixing soil** Three weeks before planting, add fully matured compost and fermented organic fertilizer to prepare.

**Planting, seeding** Plant the eggplant late April to late May. Plant daikon seeds in the summer after you prune the eggplant stems.

**Thinning** Pluck daikon several times, a little at a time, so that there will be a single radish per planting pit at 5–6th leaf that grows after a cotyledon.

**Adding fertilizer** Eggplants like a handful of fermented organic fertilizer twice monthly on the surface of the furrow.

**Harvesting** Harvest eggplant fruits as they grow and mature. Harvest daikon according to the preferred date of harvest for your variety. If you wait too long, they may start to crack.

### TIP

Be careful with the timing the planting of daikon seeds. If you plan to grow something in the same furrow after November, plant the daikon seeds by mid-August. The frequent rain makes it easier for the seeds to sprout, but harvest will be delayed. If you are planting daikons that are for harvesting in winter, you can plant seeds by late September.

## Let's look at the effects

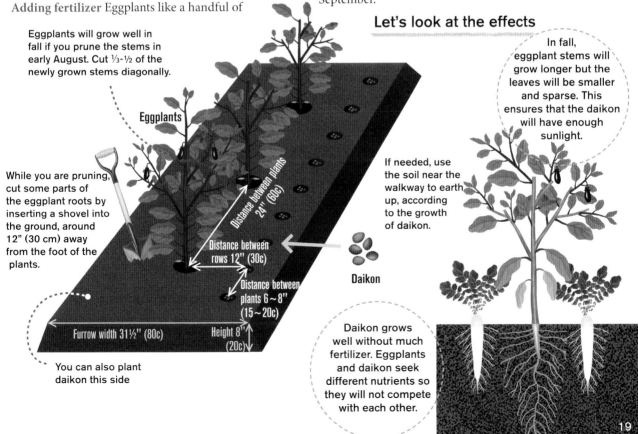

Eggplants will grow well in fall if you prune the stems in early August. Cut ⅓-½ of the newly grown stems diagonally.

Eggplants

While you are pruning, cut some parts of the eggplant roots by inserting a shovel into the ground, around 12" (30 cm) away from the foot of the plants.

Distance between plants 24" (60c)

Distance between rows 12" (30c)

Distance between plants 6~8" (15~20c)

Furrow width 31½" (80c)

Height 8" (20c)

You can also plant daikon this side

If needed, use the soil near the walkway to earth up, according to the growth of daikon.

Daikon

In fall, eggplant stems will grow longer but the leaves will be smaller and sparse. This ensures that the daikon will have enough sunlight.

Daikon grows well without much fertilizer. Eggplants and daikon seek different nutrients so they will not compete with each other.

19

# Eggplants & Parsley

## Grows healthily in the eggplant's shade, and serves as mulch

If you plant parsley in-between eggplant seedlings, both eggplants and parsley will grow well. Parsley dies fairly quickly when it is planted with tomatoes, which are from the Solanaceae (Nightshade) family. And yet eggplant, which is also a Solanaceae plant, is a great match with parsley. Both eggplant and parsley have deep roots, but somehow they do not compete against each other.

Parsley cannot handle strong sun in the summer, so it benefits from the shade created by the eggplant leaves. As parsley plants are short in height and cover the surface of the furrow in a radial pattern, they will work as mulch and moisturize the soil for the eggplants. And because parsley is an Umbelliferae family plant, it has unique scents that repel pests that are known to damage eggplants. It will also reduce the damage caused by the yellow swallowtail butterflies and plant lice.

**Application** Instead of parsley, you can also grow Italian parsley. Also, you can obtain similar effects if you plant parsley with green peppers.

### CULTIVATION PROCESS

**Selecting varieties** For both plants, any variety will work. For eggplants, using a grafted seedling will yield stronger plants. You can purchase parsley seedlings, or plant seeds mid-March to prepare seedlings in time.

**Mixing soil** Three weeks before planting, add fully matured compost and fermented organic fertilizer to prepare.

**Planting** In late April to late May, plant both eggplants and parsley.

**Adding fertilizer** For eggplants, add a handful of fermented organic fertilizer twice a month on the surface of the furrow. You do not have to worry too much about adding fertilizer for parsley.

**Straw mulching** Once parsley grows and covers the surface of the ground, it serves as mulch. If needed, cover the surface of soil using straw in other parts of the furrow.

**Harvesting** Harvest eggplant fruits as they mature. Harvest parsley from the outer leaves, as they grow bigger. Once the harvesting period is over, cut the eggplant stem at the base and give a lot of sunlight to parsley starting towards the end of the fall. You can keep harvesting the parsley leaves until spring, before the flower stalks start growing.

### TIP

Harvest parsley from the outer leaves. Since it slows down the growth if you harvest them way too often, keep at least ten leaves at all times. This will also improve the effects of repelling pests for the eggplants.

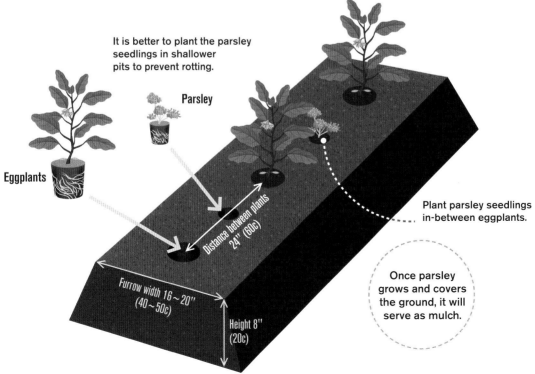

It is better to plant the parsley seedlings in shallower pits to prevent rotting.

Parsley

Eggplants

Distance between plants 24" (60c)

Furrow width 16 ~ 20" (40 ~ 50c)

Height 8" (20c)

Plant parsley seedlings in-between eggplants.

Once parsley grows and covers the ground, it will serve as mulch.

# Eggplants & Garlic Chives

## Prevents soil-borne disease using the antibiotic substance releasing antagonistic bacteria

Alliaceae family plants such as garlic chives have bacteria called *burkholderia gladioli*, which effectively reduces the amount of antagonistic bacteria in the soil.

Similar to the case of tomatoes and garlic chives (see p. 15), as eggplants also grow deep roots, plant garlic chives closely together to enhance the effect of preventing diseases. As garlic chives are a mono-cotyledonous plant and eggplants are dicotyledon, they are genetically different and therefore will not be competing against each other for nutrients.

**Application** You can apply this method of using garlic chives as a pairing with other Solanaceae family plants (see p. 15, 23).

## CULTIVATION PROCESS

**Selecting varieties** No specific eggplant variety is needed, but it's more effective to grow your own seedlings than to use grafted ones, which are less immune to diseases. You can either buy garlic chive seedlings or plant seeds mid-September to mid-October in the previous year to grow seedlings.

**Mixing soil** Three weeks before planting, add fully matured compost and fermented organic fertilizer to prepare.

**Planting** When pairing eggplants with garlic chives, plant both in late April to late May.

**Mulch usage** As eggplants hate dehydration, it is recommended to use mulch to keep the soil moist. If the ground temperature is high enough during the first stage, growth may be further enhanced. Straw is an effective mulch for keeping plants moist.

**Adding fertilizer** For eggplants, add a handful of fermented organic fertilizer twice a month on the surface of the furrow.

**Harvesting** Harvest eggplant fruits as they mature. Once garlic chive leaves grow, harvest the leaves at around 2" (5 cm) above the base. In fall, garlic chives will start growing flower stalks—cut the flower stalks quickly to prevent leaves from hardening. If you harvest garlic chives regularly, you can enjoy soft leaves year round.

## TIP

Garlic chives grow and split into tillers. If you plan to use garlic chives for pairing with another plant after harvesting eggplants, replant the garlic chives elsewhere so they can be used the following year.

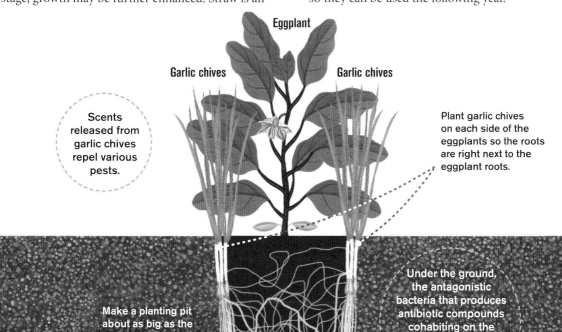

Eggplant

Garlic chives

Garlic chives

Scents released from garlic chives repel various pests.

Plant garlic chives on each side of the eggplants so the roots are right next to the eggplant roots.

Make a planting pit about as big as the size of the eggplant's root clump.

Under the ground, the antagonistic bacteria that produces antibiotic compounds cohabiting on the garlic chive roots decreases the amount of pathogenic bacteria.

# Green Peppers & Nasturtium

## Banker plants attracting natural enemies of pest insects

Nasturtium, also known as Kinrenka in Japan, is an annual plant that's cultivated in flower beds and pots. If planted in rich soil, nasturtium grows well without much effort. It flowers for all the way from May to October, except for the mid-summer when temperatures are at their highest. Flowers and leaves have a slight spiciness and tartness, and they can be used as herbs, added to salad, or cooked.

Nasturtium will be used as green pepper's banker plant (trap plant). Plant them in the corners of the furrow, or grow them all together near the walkway or the edge of the furrow. The scent of nasturtium will repel plant lice. Nasturtium can also reduce the damage caused by pests such as spider mites and thrips to the green peppers, by attracting the pests and taking them on, thereby protecting the peppers. **Application** It is also effective to cultivate sweet green peppers, peppers or eggplants together.

### CULTIVATION PROCESS

**Selecting varieties** Neither plant needs to be a specific variety. Nasturtium seedlings can be purchased in garden centers, or they can be grown from seeds if you plant the seeds in mid-March to late April.

**Mixing soil** Three weeks before planting, add fully matured compost and fermented organic fertilizer to prepare.

**Planting** Plant nasturtium in late April to late May. Plant them on a corner of the furrow, on the side of the furrow or on the walkways.

**Adding fertilizer** For green peppers, add a handful of fermented organic fertilizer twice a month on the surface of the furrow. You do not have to worry about adding fertilizer for nasturtium.

**Straw mulching** Green peppers have relatively shallow roots that are easy to damage through dehydration or high temperature—use straw mulch to moisturize the soil and to prevent the ground temperature from rising.

**Harvesting** Harvest green peppers as they mature. You can harvest nasturtium flowers and leaves in small amounts and add them to salads. Nasturtium seeds can be pickled.

### TIP

If you harvest Nasturtium from the tips, you can grow them short and use them as mulch. Nasturtium does not take well to midsummer heat; however, if you cut it low in late July, it will survive the high humidity. It will also be easier for nasturtium to survive the summer if it's grown in the shade of a companion plant's leaves.

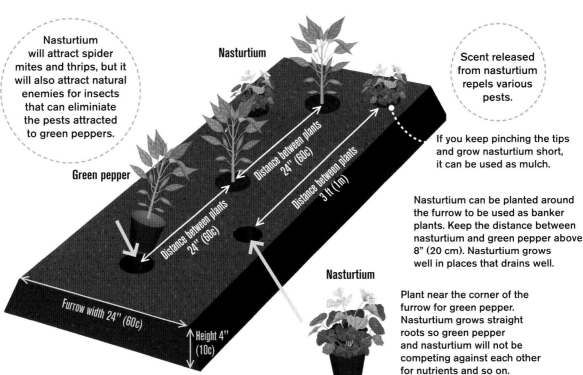

Nasturtium will attract spider mites and thrips, but it will also attract natural enemies for insects that can eliminiate the pests attracted to green peppers.

Nasturtium

Scent released from nasturtium repels various pests.

Green pepper

Distance between plants 24" (60c)

Distance between plants 24" (60c)

Distance between plants 3 ft (1m)

If you keep pinching the tips and grow nasturtium short, it can be used as mulch.

Nasturtium can be planted around the furrow to be used as banker plants. Keep the distance between nasturtium and green pepper above 8" (20 cm). Nasturtium grows well in places that drains well.

Nasturtium

Furrow width 24" (60c)

Height 4" (10c)

Plant near the corner of the furrow for green pepper. Nasturtium grows straight roots so green pepper and nasturtium will not be competing against each other for nutrients and so on.

# Green Peppers & Garlic Chives

Prevents disease   Repels pests

## Prevents soil-borne disease using the antibiotic substance releasing antagonistic bacteria

One of the major soil-borne diseases that affect green pepper is phytophthora blight. If dark spots appear on the stems and leaves, your peppers may be infected. As the disease advances, stems and leaves shrivel and the plant may die shortly thereafter. The disease is caused by the antagonistic bacteria in the soil, and it happens often when Solanaceae family plants are cultivated in the same plot continuously.

Similar to tomatoes and eggplants, planting garlic chives can reduce the risk of soil-borne diseases thanks to the bacteria called *burkholderia gladioli,* which lives on garlic chive roots.

Green pepper grows its roots relatively wide compared to tomatoes and eggplants; however, it is recommended to use garlic chives that grow deep roots. It is also recommended to plant the garlic chives so that their roots touch each other under the green pepper roots.

**Application** Planting with garlic chives works for varieties similar to green pepper, such as sweet green pepper, pepper, and Solanaceae plants such as tomatoes and eggplants (see p. 15, 21).

## CULTIVATION PROCESS

**Selecting varieties** Green pepper seedlings are made widely available; however, it is more effective to grow your own seedlings instead of using grafted seedlings, as they are less immune to diseases. You can either buy garlic chive seedlings or plant seeds mid-September to mid-October in the previous year to grow seedlings.

**Mixing soil** Three weeks before planting, add fully matured compost and fermented organic fertilizer to prepare.

**Planting** Plant both green pepper and garlic chives while connected to each other in late April to late May.

**Adding fertilizer** For green peppers, add a handful of fermented organic fertilizer twice a month on the surface of the furrow. You do not have to worry about adding fertilizer for garlic chives.

**Straw mulching** Green peppers have relatively shallow roots that are easy to damage due to dehydration or high temperature—use straw mulch to moisturize the soil and to prevent the ground temperature from rising.

**Harvesting** Harvest green pepper fruits as they grow and mature. Once garlic chive leaves grow, harvest the leaves at around 2" (5 cm) above the base. In fall, garlic chives will start growing flower stalks—cut the flower stalks quickly to prevent leaves from hardening. If you harvest garlic chives regularly, you can eat soft leaves all around the year.

## TIP

Garlic chives grow and split into tillers. If you plan to use garlic chives for planting with another plant after harvesting green pepper, replant the garlic chives elsewhere so they can be used the following year.

Green pepper

Garlic chives

Garlic chives

Plant garlic chives on each side of the green pepper so the that plants' roots are right next to each other.

Scents released from garlic chives repel various pests.

Dig a pit planting about the size of the green pepper's root clump.

Green pepper roots grow relatively wide, but it is more effective if you plant garlic chives near the foot of the green pepper plants.

Under the ground, the antagonistic bacteria that produces antibiotic compounds cohabiting on the garlic chive roots decreases the amount of pathogenic bacteria.

# Cucumbers & Chinese Yams

Efficient use of space  Speeds up growth

## Enhance growth by pairing two plants that prefer each other's least favorite nutrients

When you plant Chinese yam next to cucumber, it grows very healthily while spreading its vines into the net or trellis.

Organic substances are broken into ammonia nitrogen and later gradually become nitrate nitrogen. Chinese yam likes ammonia nitrogen. If Chinese yam absorbs too much nitrate nitrogen, vitamin C in the yam will decrease. In contrast, cucumber does not like raw organic substances or ammonia nitrogen. Each of these plants likes and absorbs the types of nutrients the other plant dislikes. Thus, pairing them accelerates the growth of each vegetable.

### CULTIVATION PROCESS

**Selecting varieties** Cucumber does not have to be a specific variety; however, it will grow stronger if it is a grafted seedling. It is recommended to choose a Chinese yam variety that produces long yams.

**Mixing soil** Three weeks before planting, add fully matured compost and fermented organic fertilizer to prepare.

**Planting** Plant both cucumber and Chinese yam in late April to late May.

**Straw mulching** Neither cucumber nor Chinese yam can handle dehydration or high temperatures. Lay down straw mulch after planting.

**Adding fertilizer** For cucumber, add fermented organic fertilizer every three weeks, lightly mixing it with soil on the ground. As cucumber grows shallow roots, change the placement of fertilizer according to the cucumber's growth stage. For example, you can add fertilizer at the base, then change its position to the side of the furrow, then to the walkway. You do not have to add fertilizer for Chinese yam, as they grow well even in soil with low nutrition.

**Harvesting** Harvest cucumbers as they mature. Once cucumber leaves start to die, cut the plant from the base and discard it. Keep growing Chinese yam until November, when they are harvested.

### TIP

Chinese yam must be attached to the net or trellis. Yams will grows bigger if the vines are guided to grow upwards. Growth will be less if the vines are on the ground, as bulbils will start sprouting, directing the plant's energies elsewhere.

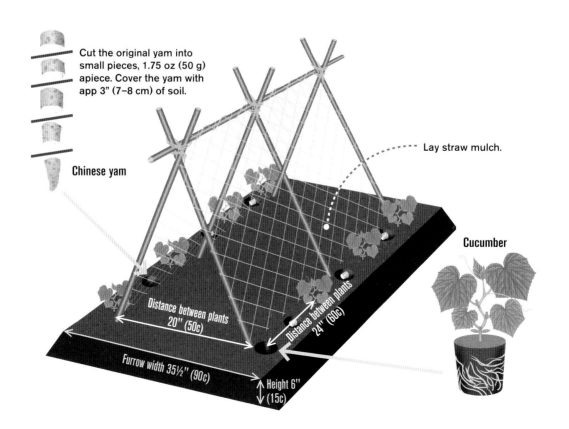

Cut the original yam into small pieces, 1.75 oz (50 g) apiece. Cover the yam with app 3" (7–8 cm) of soil.

Chinese yam

Lay straw mulch.

Cucumber

Distance between plants 20" (50c)

Distance between plants 24" (60c)

Furrow width 35½" (90c)

Height 6" (15c)

# Let's look at the effects

**Efficient use of resources**

The same net or trellis used to support the cucumbers can be used to grow Chinese yam.

**Simultaneous management**

Staw mulch benefits both plants, reducing your efforts to keep them hydrated.

**Each prefers the other's least favorite nutrients**

Cucumber likes nitrate nitrogen, and dislikes raw organic substances or immature compost, which can kill the roots. Chinese yam likes ammonia nitrogen and the quality of yam drops when there is too much of nitrate nitrogen.

# Cucumbers & Scallions

## Prevent repeated cultivation damage using an ages-old farming technique

In Japan's Tochigi Prefecture, it has long been known anecdotally that planting scallions near white-flowered gourd (also called bottle gourd) stops diseases such as fusarium wilt. After this was investigated scientifically, it was discovered that scallions have the antibiotic bacteria *burkholderia gladioli*, which decreases antagonistic bacteria in the soil. It was also discovered that scallions have the same effect on Cucurbitaceae plants such as white-flowered gourd and cucumber, as well as Solanaceae family plants.

As cucumber grows shallow roots, scallions that grow roots in the same general area can be paired in the same way as garlic chives.

**Application** You can use scallions for Cucurbitaceae family plants that grow shallow roots, like pumpkins and melons (see p. 30, 34). Alternatives to scallions are green onion and chives.

### CULTIVATION PROCESS

**Selecting varieties** Any variety can work for both plants. It is more effective to grow a seedling than to use a grafted seedling. You can either plant store-bought seedlings, or plant seeds beforehand to prepare seedlings.

**Mixing soil** Three weeks before planting, add fully matured compost and fermented organic fertilizer to prepare.

**Planting** Plant both plants in late April to late May.

**Mulching** As cucumber cannot handle heat or dehydration, lay down straw littler after planting.

**Adding fertilizer** For cucumber, add a handful of fermented organic fertilizer once every three weeks. Lightly mix the fertilizer with soil. As the roots grow near the surface of the ground, change the placement of fertilizer according to the plant's growth stage. You do not have to worry about adding fertilizer for scallion plants.

**Harvesting** Harvest cucumbers as they mature. Harvest scallions after the end of fall.

### TIP

It is important not to let the plants to fall prey to disease, especially during their first stage of growth. Scallion roots grow while touching the cucumber roots, which can prevent diseases.

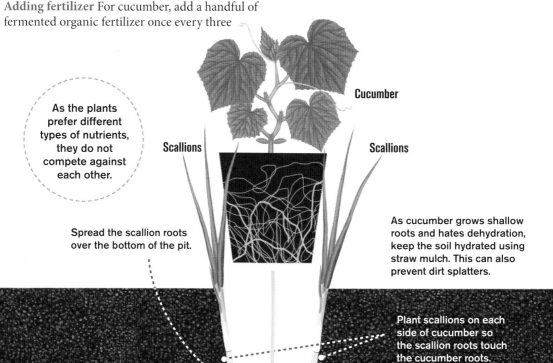

Cucumber

Scallions

Scallions

As the plants prefer different types of nutrients, they do not compete against each other.

Spread the scallion roots over the bottom of the pit.

As cucumber grows shallow roots and hates dehydration, keep the soil hydrated using straw mulch. This can also prevent dirt splatters.

Plant scallions on each side of cucumber so the scallion roots touch the cucumber roots.

# Cucumbers & Wheat

## A disease common to cucumber is powdery mildew

To prevent this, you can grow wheat as a "living mulch" as you scatter wheat grains around the furrow.

Wheat acts as a trap and a habitat for mycoparasites that can kill powdery mildew bacteria. This can hugely reduce the risk of powdery mildew affecting cucumber.

Wheat suffers from its own list of pests, such as plant lice, but these will not affect cucumber. Rather, the wheat will become a home for ladybugs and other insects that can kill pests.

**Application** You can also apply this method to zucchini, pumpkin and watermelon as well as cucumber. Wheat as a living mulch is also useful for plants such as eggplants and green pepper.

### CULTIVATION PROCESS

**Selecting varieties** Cucumber can be any variety; however, a grafted seedling will yield stronger growth. For wheat, barley is useful, as it will not grow ears if planted in this season.

**Mixing soil** Three weeks before planting, add fully matured compost and fermented organic fertilizer to prepare.

**Planting** Scatter wheat grains on the furrow and on the walkways after you plant cucumber in mid-May. As birds love the grains, lightly cover the grains with soil using a rake.

**Adding fertilizer** For cucumber, add a handful of fermented organic fertilizer once every three weeks. Lightly mix the fertilizer with soil. As the roots grow near the surface of the ground, change the placement of fertilizer according to the plant's growth stage.

**Harvesting** Harvest cucumbers when they mature. Wheat will die in summer due to the heat.

### TIP

When the wheat dies in the summer, use the dead leaves and stems as mulch rather than discarding them. When growing another plant afterwards, you can use them as green manure if you till them into the soil.

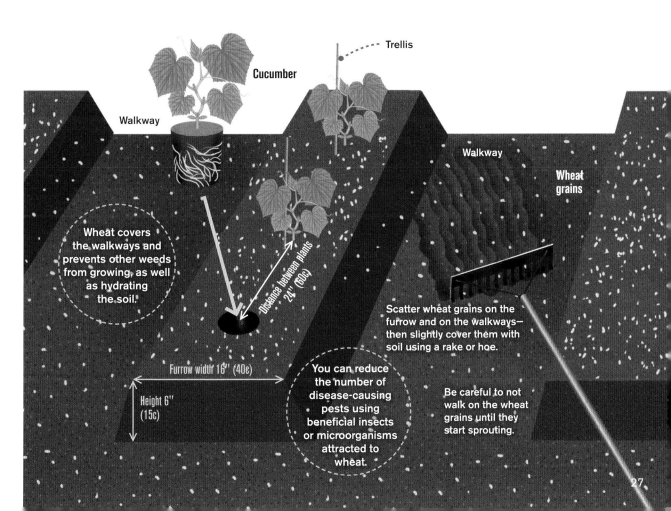

Trellis

Cucumber

Walkway

Walkway

Wheat grains

Wheat covers the walkways and prevents other weeds from growing, as well as hydrating the soil.

Distance between plants 24" (60c)

Scatter wheat grains on the furrow and on the walkways—then slightly cover them with soil using a rake or hoe.

Furrow width 16" (40c)

Height 6" (15c)

You can reduce the number of disease-causing pests using beneficial insects or microorganisms attracted to wheat.

Be careful to not walk on the wheat grains until they start sprouting.

# Pumpkins & Corn

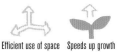
Efficient use of space   Speeds up growth

## Use space efficiently by growing plants that grow in different directions

Pumpkins grow vines horizontally and thus require a wide space for cultivation. Also, as pumpkins have wind-pollinated flowers, it is common to grow a lot of seedlings to make pollination easier. Mixing corn and pumpkin allows you to grow both of them on the same furrow, as they grow in different directions.

Corn can handle some level of dehydration and hot weather, and likes sunlight. Pumpkin, by contrast, can grow in places with some shade. As pumpkins grow and cover the foot of corn plants, they also function as mulch, which hydrates the soil and prevents weeds from growing.

Also, corn likes ammonia nitrogen, whereas pumpkin likes nitrate nitrogen. Corn first absorbs ammonia nitrogen, and since ammonia nitrogen later turns into nitrate nitrogen, the amount of nitrate nitrogen can be limited. This will prevent the overgrowing of pumpkin vines.

**Application** Instead of pumpkins, you may plant watermelons or gourds.

### CULTIVATION PROCESS

**Selecting varieties** Any variety can work for both plants.

**Preparing seedlings** It takes 3–4 weeks for both plants to grow from seeds to seedlings. Plant three seeds in a plastic pot, and crop the sprouts when there are 2–3 leaves to grow one plant per pot. Grow the plant until it has four leaves. Plant one pumpkin seed per plastic pot. Plant the seedlings when there are 4–5 leaves.

**Mixing soil** Three weeks before planting, add fully matured compost and fermented organic fertilizer to prepare.

**Planting** Plant both plants in early May to late May.

**Nipping** Once pumpkin grows two side vines, nip the tip of the original vine.

**Adding fertilizer** If the soil is poor, add fertilizer once or twice. Add a handful of fermented organic fertilizer near corn, and lightly mix the fertilizer with soil. You do not have to add fertilizer for pumpkin.

**Harvesting** Corn can be harvested in about 60 days. The ideal harvest period for pumpkin is 50 days after female flowers bloom.

### TIP

Though pumpkin grows well when it's warmer, corn sustains pest damage if planted too late. If you plant on the early side, protect the pumpkin seedlings from the cold or strong wind at least until they become more mature.

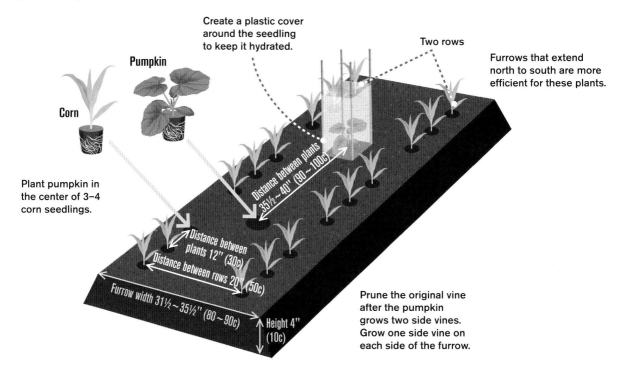

# Let's look at the effects

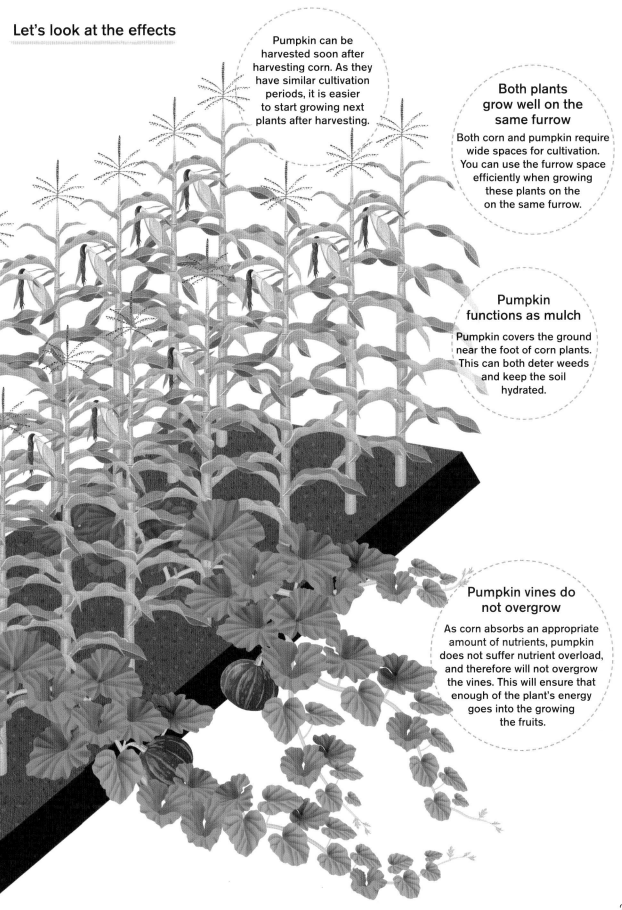

Pumpkin can be harvested soon after harvesting corn. As they have similar cultivation periods, it is easier to start growing next plants after harvesting.

## Both plants grow well on the same furrow

Both corn and pumpkin require wide spaces for cultivation. You can use the furrow space efficiently when growing these plants on the on the same furrow.

## Pumpkin functions as mulch

Pumpkin covers the ground near the foot of corn plants. This can both deter weeds and keep the soil hydrated.

## Pumpkin vines do not overgrow

As corn absorbs an appropriate amount of nutrients, pumpkin does not suffer nutrient overload, and therefore will not overgrow the vines. This will ensure that enough of the plant's energy goes into the growing the fruits.

# Pumpkins & Scallions

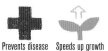

## Prevents soil-borne diseases and bears high quality fruits

Although pumpkin is usually immune to diseases, it can sometimes suffer from soil-borne diseases such as blight. When pumpkin is affected by diseases, the plant may die in mid-growth or the fruits will be damaged if left on the vine to mature.

Similar to cucumbers, you can plant scallions with pumpkin. This will reduce the risk of diseases because scallion roots release antibiotic bacteria that can kill antagonistic bacteria. Also, scallion can absorb any excess fertilizer, thereby preventing pumpkin vines from overgrowing, allowing the pumpkin to produce high quality fruits.

**Application** You can plant scallions with cucumber, watermelon and muskmelon (see p. 24, 32, 34).

### CULTIVATION PROCESS

**Selecting varieties** Any variety can work for both plants. You can either plant store-bought seedlings, or plant seeds beforehand to prepare seedlings.

**Mixing soil** Three weeks before planting, add fully matured compost and fermented organic fertilizer to prepare.

**Planting** Plant both plants in early to late May. Pumpkin grows well if you make a plastic cover around the plant to protect it from the cold and strong wind.

**Nipping** Once pumpkin grows 2–3 side vines, nip the tip of the original vine.

**Adding fertilizer** Not necessary.

**Harvesting** The ideal harvest period for pumpkin is 50 days after female flowers bloom.

### TIP

If you are planting pumpkin to be harvested in fall, plant pumpkin seeds afterwards in late July.

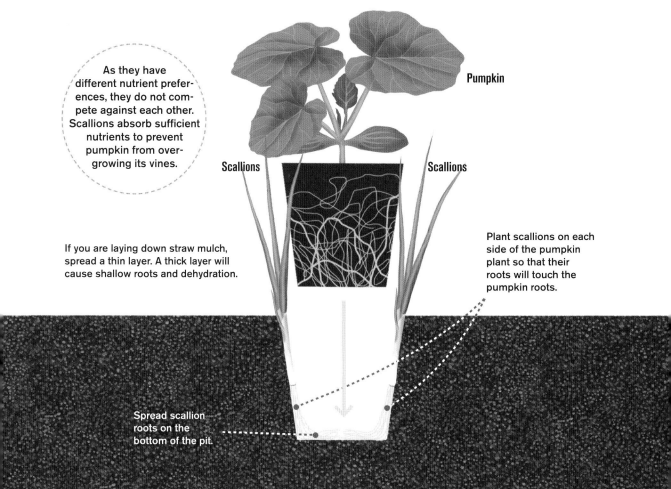

As they have different nutrient preferences, they do not compete against each other. Scallions absorb sufficient nutrients to prevent pumpkin from overgrowing its vines.

Pumpkin

Scallions

Scallions

If you are laying down straw mulch, spread a thin layer. A thick layer will cause shallow roots and dehydration.

Plant scallions on each side of the pumpkin plant so that their roots will touch the pumpkin roots.

Spread scallion roots on the bottom of the pit.

# Pumpkins & Barley

Speeds up growth    Prevents disease

## Barley stalks support the pumpkins' vines

In order for a pumpkin to grow, the vine should have more than ten leaves past the point where female flower grows. If there are more than fifteen leaves, it is possible to grow two pumpkins on a single vine.

To grow a lot of leaves, the soil where the vine is grown should be kept hydrated with straw mulch. This makes it easy for vines to grow roots. Growing pumpkins alongside barley eliminates the task of laying straw mulch.

Barley, if planted in spring to early summer, will not grow tall but will grow in radial directions, covering up the ground. As this will hydrate the soil and prevent weeds from growing, the pumpkin roots will spread more easily. In addition, pumpkin tendrils will grasp barley leaves in order to stabilize their position. Thus, vines and leaves will grow well, resulting in delicious pumpkin fruits.

**Application** As an alternative to pumpkin, you can also use watermelon and cucumber varieties that grow short and wide. You can also use oats or white clover in place of barley. Barley that is planted in the summer tends to grow tall so you'll need to keep it near the ground by tamping it down.

### CULTIVATION PROCESS

**Selecting varieties** For pumpkin, any variety will work. You can buy barley designed to be used as living mulch.

**Mixing soil** Three weeks before planting, add fully matured compost and fermented organic fertilizer to prepare.

**Planting, seeding** After planting pumpkin seedlings in May, make a plastic cover for protection. Scatter barley grains around the furrow and on the walkways. Lightly cover the grains with soil by raking.

**Nipping** Once pumpkin grows 2–3 side vines, nip the tip of the original vine.

**Adding fertilizer** Not necessary.

**Harvesting** The ideal harvest period for pumpkin is 50 days after female flowers bloom. Barley will die in summer due to the heat.

### TIP

If you are planting pumpkin to be harvested in fall, you can use the dead barley leaves after summer. After harvesting pumpkins, mix the dead leaves with soil to use them as green manure.

Barley can contract powdery mildew, but it will attract mycoparasites that can eliminiate powdery mildew bacteria on pumpkin.

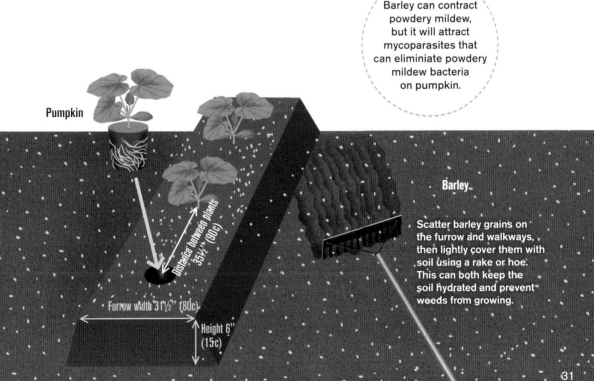

Pumpkin

Distance between plants 35½" (90c)

Furrow width 31½" (80c)

Height 6" (15c)

Barley

Scatter barley grains on the furrow and walkways, then lightly cover them with soil using a rake or hoe. This can both keep the soil hydrated and prevent weeds from growing.

# Watermelons & Scallions

## Root nodule bacteria on scallion roots kills antagonistic bacteria and makes watermelon more immune to diseases

Just like other Cucurbitaceae family plants, watermelon occasionally suffers from fusarium wilt, a common vascular wilt disease that ultimately prevents vines from properly conducting water and nutrients. As the antagonistic bacteria stay alive for a long time, something needs to be done to kill them off.

If you plant scallions and watermelon together, the antibiotic bacteria on scallion roots can kill the antagonistic bacteria, making it harder for watermelon to contract diseases. Watermelon grows deep roots and has few side roots. While scallions grow shallow roots, their roots are adequate to kill the antagonistic bacteria, since the bacteria dwell in the shallower area of the soil.

**Application** You can apply this method to cucumber, pumpkin, muskmelon, and gourd (see p. 26, 30, 34).

### CULTIVATION PROCESS

**Selecting varieties** Any variety can work for both plants. You can either plant store-bought seedlings, or plant seeds beforehand to prepare seedlings.

**Mixing soil** Three weeks before planting, add fully matured compost and fermented organic fertilizer to prepare a furrow with a "saddle."

**Planting** Plant both plants in mid-May to late May. Watermelon grows well if you make a plastic cover around the plant to protect it from the cold and strong wind.

**Straw mulching** Cover the whole furrow with straw mulch. Instead of laying a thick layer, make it just enough that you can still see the soil from above.

**Nipping** Nip the tip of the parent vine after 5–6 nodes. If the fruits are large, consider clipping fruits to grow just a couple per vine, to allow for better quality.

**Adding fertilizer** Once the fruit becomes as big as a fist, add a handful of fermented organic fertilizer near the base.

**Harvesting** Harvest according to the determined harvest date of the specific variety. You can also check on the timing by lightly tapping on the fruit and listening to the sound. A full/hollow sound indicates ripeness, whereas a deep/dull sound means the fruit isn't quite ready.

### TIP

It is important to not allow the plants to fall prey to disease during their first stage of growth. Scallion roots grow while touching the watermelon roots, which can prevent diseases.

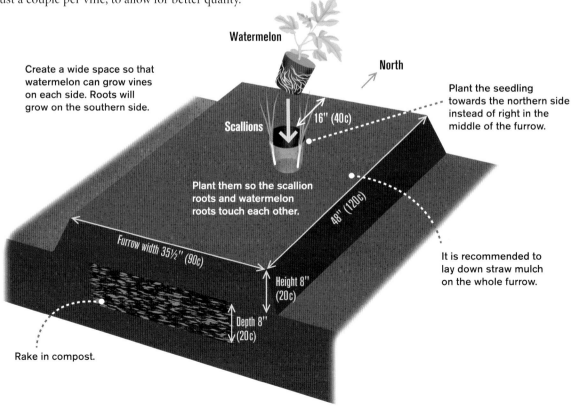

Watermelon

North

Create a wide space so that watermelon can grow vines on each side. Roots will grow on the southern side.

Plant the seedling towards the northern side instead of right in the middle of the furrow.

Scallions

16" (40c)

Plant them so the scallion roots and watermelon roots touch each other.

48" (120c)

Furrow width 35½" (90c)

Height 8" (20c)

It is recommended to lay down straw mulch on the whole furrow.

Depth 8" (20c)

Rake in compost.

# Watermelons & Purslane

Speeds up growth

## Use deep-rooted weeds to enhance watermelon roots' functions

Watermelons are native to deserts in tropical and savanna areas. As these are dry regions, watermelons grow deep, straight roots that absorb water like a pump. Like watermelon, purslane has deep, straight roots, and planting it with watermelon it can help the watermelon roots absorb water. As a result, watermelon seedlings will grow well, and its vines and leaves will perform excellent photosynthesis. This yields watermelon fruit that is sweet and succulent.

**Application** Alternatives to purslane include green pak choi or komatsuna (Japanese mustard spinach).

### CULTIVATION PROCESS

**Selecting varieties** Watermelon can be any variety. Purslane seeds can be purchased.

**Mixing soil** Three weeks before planting, add fully matured compost and fermented organic fertilizer to prepare a furrow with a "saddle" (See illustration on p. 32).

**Planting** Plant watermelon in mid-to-late May.

**Nipping** Nip the tip of the parent vine after 5–6 nodes. If the fruits are large, consider clipping fruits to grow just a couple per vine, to allow for better quality.

**Adding fertilizer** Once the fruit becomes as big as a fist, add a handful of fermented organic fertilizer near the base.

**Harvesting** For harvesting watermelons, see p. 32. Purslane is ready for harvest at roughly 60 days after sowing.

### TIP

It is better not to lay down straw mulch if purslane does not grow well in your area. Otherwise, lay the straw mulch as thinly as possible to encourage purslane to grow.

## Let's look at the effects

You can also grow watermelon, scallions and purslane together.

Watermelon

**Watermelon grows leaves well and develops sweet fruits**

As the watermelon roots grow deep, vines above the ground will also grow well. Once there are enough leaves for photosynthesis, the fruit gets sweeter.

**Purslane helps watermelon with absorbing water**

Purslane is also a straight-rooted plant. As the roots will absorb water from the deeper side of soil when the surface is dry, they will help watermelon absorb water and develop succulent fruits.

**Functions as mulch**

As purslane spreads and covers the surface of the ground, and can handle the heat and dehydration, it can function as mulch.

Purslane

Scallions

**Watermelon roots grow deep**

As purslane roots spread, it becomes easier for the watermelon roots to have better exposure to air. As a result, watermelon will grow deep roots. Purslane roots will also improve water drainage.

# Muskmelons & Scallions

## Prevent diseases like fusarium wilt using root nodule bacteria on the scallion roots

Just like any other Cucurbitaceae family plant, muskmelon also often suffers from diseases such as fusarium wilt. Grafted seedlings are more immune to diseases; however, you can grow your own muskmelon seedlings from scratch if you pair them with scallions. A type of bacteria called *burkholderia gladioli* that live on scallion roots can kill the antagonistic bacteria and greatly reduce the risk of diseases. Since muskmelons grow shallow roots, pair them with scallions that also grow shallow roots.

**Application** You can plant cucumber, pumpkin, and gourds as alternatives to muskmelons, as all of these plants grow shallow roots (see p. 26, 30, 32). In place of scallions, you can also grow chives.

### CULTIVATION PROCESS

**Selecting varieties** Any variety can work for both plants. You can either plant store-bought seedlings, or plant seeds beforehand to prepare seedlings.

**Mixing soil** Three weeks before planting, add fully matured compost and fermented organic fertilizer to prepare.

**Planting** Plant both plants in early May to late May.

**Straw mulching** As muskmelon roots do not like heat or dehydration, lay down straw mulch after planting.

**Nipping** Nip the tip of the original vine at 5–6 nodes, and let two side vines grow.

**Adding fertilizer** For muskmelon, add a handful of fermented organic fertilizer every three weeks. Lightly mix the fertilizer with soil. To avoid damaging the roots that grow near the vines, place the fertilizer near the tip of the vines. You do not have to add fertilizer to scallions.

**Harvesting** Harvest muskmelons after the fruit surface begins to have veins, or if the fruit becomes fragrant. After harvesting muskmelons, transplant the scallions to a different spot and continue growing them until the end of fall.

### TIP

It is important to not allow the plants to fall prey to disease during their first stage of growth. Scallion roots grow while touching the muskmelon roots, which can prevent diseases.

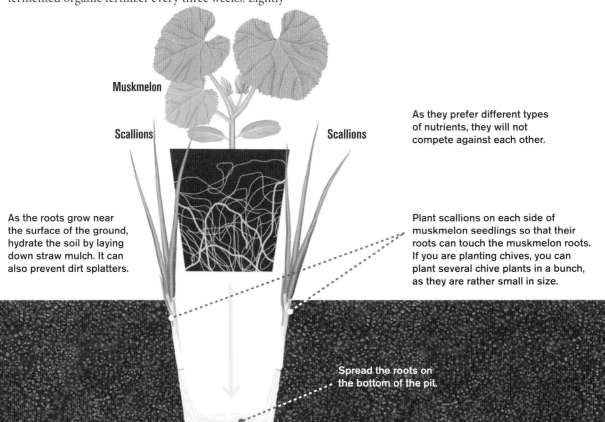

Muskmelon

Scallions

Scallions

As they prefer different types of nutrients, they will not compete against each other.

As the roots grow near the surface of the ground, hydrate the soil by laying down straw mulch. It can also prevent dirt splatters.

Plant scallions on each side of muskmelon seedlings so that their roots can touch the muskmelon roots. If you are planting chives, you can plant several chive plants in a bunch, as they are rather small in size.

Spread the roots on the bottom of the pit.

# Muskmelons & Foxtail Grass

Speeds up growth

Prevents disease

Repels pests

## Foxtail grass is a Poaceae weed that commonly grows between fall and spring

It grows very quickly when spring comes and develops flower spikes during May-June. It dies in the summer due to the heat. Muskmelon seedlings are planted in May, so you can use foxtail grass there if it is grown on the furrow or the walkways. Once the flower spikes start growing, cut the spikes to about 4" (10 cm). This keeps the foxtail grass youthful. It will then spread the leaves in a radial direction and cover the ground.

Muskmelon vines will attach themselves to foxtail grass leaves, and foxtail grass will prevent dirt splatters and growth of other types of weeds. In addition, foxtail grass is home to beneficial mycoparasite bacteria that can kill antagonistic bacteria that cause diseases like powdery mildew. PLEASE NOTE: Foxtails are the barbed, spiny grass awns that grow at the tops of foxtail grass stalks. These are injurious to animals, so consider scallions or chives instead of foxtail grass if you live with or near dogs and cats.
**Application** You can also use this method for pumpkins and gourds.

### CULTIVATION PROCESS

**Selecting varieties** Muskmelon does not need to be specific variety.

**Mixing soil** Foxtail grass grows well if you prepare a furrow by the end of fall. Three weeks before planting, add fully matured compost and fermented organic fertilizer to prepare.

**Pruning stems** To prevent foxtail grass from growing flower spikes, mow it down and leave 4" (10 cm) in height. Keep the foxtail grass short at all times.

**Planting** Plant muskmelon in May.

### Let's look at the effects

**Adding fertilizer** See p. 34

**Harvesting** Harvest muskmelon after the fruit surface begins to have veins, or the unique scent of muskmelon gets stronger. Foxtail grass dies in fall.

### TIP

Foxtail grass originally grow in places that used to be rice fields. If foxtail grass does not sprout, you can scatter mulch barley when planting muskmelon seedlings.

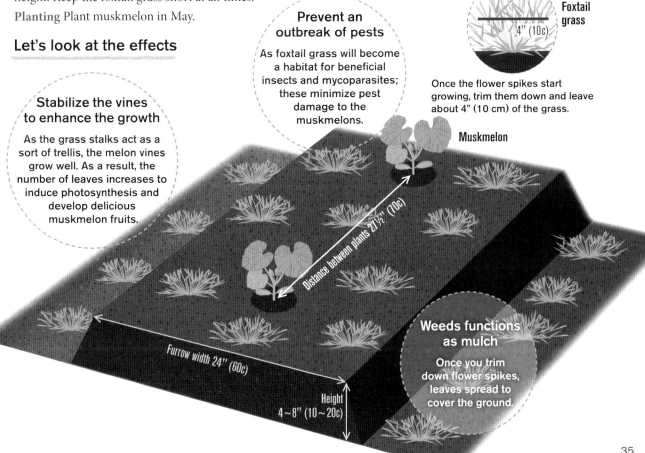

**Foxtail grass**

4" (10c)

Once the flower spikes start growing, trim them down and leave about 4" (10 cm) of the grass.

**Muskmelon**

**Prevent an outbreak of pests**

As foxtail grass will become a habitat for beneficial insects and mycoparasites; these minimize pest damage to the muskmelons.

**Stabilize the vines to enhance the growth**

As the grass stalks act as a sort of trellis, the melon vines grow well. As a result, the number of leaves increases to induce photosynthesis and develop delicious muskmelon fruits.

Distance between plants 27½" (70c)

Furrow width 24" (60c)

Height 4~8" (10~20c)

**Weeds functions as mulch**

Once you trim down flower spikes, leaves spread to cover the ground.

Tips on Mulch Cultivation

# Weeds to Keep in Your Garden

For vegetable cultivation, you may think that weeds should be removed as they grow; however, there are weeds that speed up the growth of vegetables, or some that prevent diseases and damage from repeated cultivation.

## Use weeds as a companion plant

As an agricultural book from the Edo era says, "Upper-class farmers remove weeds without seeing the weeds, middle-class farmers remove weeds after seeing the weeds, and lower-class farmers see the weeds and do not remove them." A completely weed-free farm was once considered the ideal. Weeds were—and in many ways still are—thought to be nutrients—thieves or habitats for pests.

However, vegetables were originally also naturally grown like weeds. Where they are native, they coexist with other types of plants yet still grow well. Therefore, it is possible to think of weeds as a companion plant to be used in cultivation to help the growth of vegetables.

For example, if you grow cabbage on the same farm for several years, weeds such as chickweed and aster start covering the ground to stabilize the growth of cabbage. Pumpkin grows well by attaching its vines onto weeds such as crabgrass. Watermelon grows sweet, succulent fruits if you allow native purslane to grow in your garden, as the purslane roots grow deep and become a water source.

## Also useful for preventing repeated cultivation damage or removing disease-causing pests

When you grow peas repeatedly, the substance released from the roots remains in the soil, making it extremely hard for plants to grow. However, if you allow an appropriate amount of weeds to grow, you can somehow stop the occurrence of damage from repeated cultivation.

Also, the number of types of pests that are attracted to both vegetables and weeds is limited. Rather, weeds play the role of "banker plant" by attracting beneficial insects that kill the pests on vegetable plants.

Similarly, weeds can also prevent diseases. As powdery mildew has different types of bacteria depending on the seed or plant species, powdery mildew on weeds will not affect the vegetables. Rather, you can increase the number of bacteria that can kill the bacteria that cause powdery mildew on vegetables such as tomatoes, pumpkin, muskmelon and zucchini.

**Examples of mulch cultivation**

**Cabbage & Chickweed**
Chickweed covers the ground around cabbage to keep the temperature and humidity of the soil. Chickweed mulch can happen after years of repeated cultivation of cabbage.

**Komatsuna & Lambsquarters**
Lambsquarters comes from a different plant family, so it can repel the pests attracted to Komatsuna (Japanese mustard spinach), a Brassicaceae plant.

**Tomato & Mugwort**
Mugwort grows in groups on the walkways between tomato patches. It can be used as a banker plant to attract beneficial insects that can kill pests such as plant lice, spider mites and thrips.

### Clover
Also known as white clover. It grows creeping stems that cover up the ground. As it is a Fabaceae plant, it can slowly enrich the soil. It commonly gets powdery mildew, and then attracts mycoparasites that can prevent powdery mildew on Cucurbitaceae vegetables and so on.

### Shepherd's purse
A Brassicaceae weed and medicinal herb. It trhives in relatively rich soil that is slightly acidic. This type of weed can induce the disintegration of raw organic substance in soil due to its rhizosphere microorganism.

### Foxtail grass
A Gramineae weed that grows in most climate conditions. This type of weed is often used for mulch cultivation to allow muskmelon to grow its vines around them.

### Lambsquarters
A weed that belongs to the Chenopodiaceae family—same plant family as spinach. It can be found growing from spring to fall. As it grows in groups and has deep roots, you can use it as a banker plant.

### Chickweed
A Caryophyllaceae weed. It can be found growing on rich soil. It grows well in slightly acidic soil and can cover up the ground. It works well with Brassicaceae plants such as cabbage and broccoli.

### Mugwort
Asteraceae. It spreads stems underground and prevents other types of weeds. A plant with medicinal properties, it has a unique scent and slightly bitter taste, great in soups or mixed with rice. It can not only repel pests but also increase the number of natural enemies of plant lice, spider mites and thrips.

### Japanese nigglewort
Labiatae. It can be found growing next to chickweed from fall to spring. After spring starts, they start having cute flowers. It can be used for cultivation of wintering vegetables like cabbage.

### Purslane
Portulacaceae. Good in salads or pesto, or steamed. It spreads fleshy leaves and cover the ground, which hydrates the soil. Also, it grows deep roots and become a pathway for air and water. A similar species called flower purslane is grown as an ornamental plant.

### Wood sorrel
Oxalidaceae weed with creeping stems. It bears fruits after its flowers bloom, and then the wind spreads its seeds. It can encourage natural enemies of spider mites.

### Plantain
Plantaginaceae. A very hardy weed, it regrows even after being trampled underfoot. As it often suffers from powdery mildew, it can prevent powdery mildew on grapes if you plant them under the grape trees.

# Corn & Vine Type Green Beans

Speeds up growth    Efficient use of space

## Enhance your plants' growth by allowing vines to attach themselves to corn stems

Mixed planting of corn and green beans has been practiced among Native Americans for centuries. In the western and mountainous areas of Japan, this method has also been used, with peas or velvet beans in place of green beans.

The biggest advantage to this pairing is the efficient use of space. If you plant green bean seeds in-between corn seedlings, green beans will sprout and grow their vines around corn stems. Corn requires a lot of fertilizer, and green bean roots release natural fertilizer from the root nodule bacteria that convert nitrogen in the atmosphere into nutrients. In this way, green beans improve the growth of corn plants. **Application** You can also plant velvet beans or fall-harvest peas as alternatives to green beans.

## CULTIVATION PROCESS

**Selecting varieties** Choose a sweetcorn variety. You can choose any vine type of green beans. It's good to use varieties that are native to your area.

**Preparing seedlings** Plant three corn seeds per plastic pot, and pluck out the sprouts once it has 2–3 leaves, so that there is only one plant per pot. Grow it until the plant has four leaves. It takes about 3–4 weeks before it is ready to plant.

**Mixing soil** Three weeks before planting, add fully matured compost and fermented organic fertilizer to prepare.

**Planting, seeding** The planting season is mid-April to mid-May. Once you are finished planting the corn seedlings, plant three green bean seeds between the seedlings. You can do this immediately after you plant the corn or a day or two after. You can also grow green beans with corn when you plant corn seedlings that have been grown from seeds in late July to early August.

**Adding fertilizer** Usually not necessary. If there is too much fertilizer, bean vines will overgrow and pods will not develop fully.

**Earthing up** Once corn develops lateral roots near the base, earth up.

**Harvesting** You can harvest corn about 60–70 days after planting. You can also start harvesting green beans around the same time. If you start harvesting green beans relatively early, you can continue harvesting green beans for a longer period of time.

## TIP

If you plant green beans too early, or add too much fertilizer, it may prevent corn from getting adequate sunlight. Therefore, plant green bean seeds up to 1–2 weeks before planting corn.

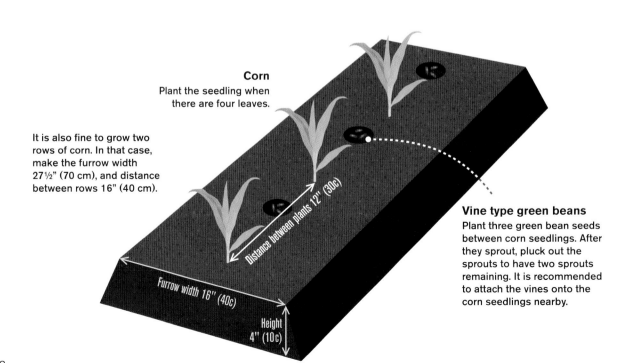

**Corn**
Plant the seedling when there are four leaves.

It is also fine to grow two rows of corn. In that case, make the furrow width 27½" (70 cm), and distance between rows 16" (40 cm).

Distance between plants 12" (30c)

Furrow width 16" (40c)

Height 4" (10c)

**Vine type green beans**
Plant three green bean seeds between corn seedlings. After they sprout, pluck out the sprouts to have two sprouts remaining. It is recommended to attach the vines onto the corn seedlings nearby.

**Corn stems serve as a trellis**

Green beans will grow the vines while attaching the vines onto the corn seedling. After harvesting corn, you can grow green beans until fall.

**Enrich the soil using root nodule bacteria**

Root nodule bacteria on green bean roots can capture nitrogen in the atmosphere and enrich the soil nearby.

# Corn & Adzuki Beans

## Similar to pairing corn with green beans, this is another combination of corn and a Fabaceae plant

Adzuki bean roots have root nodule bacteria that capture nitrogen in the atmosphere and convert it into nutrients, enriching the soil and enhancing the corn's growth. As long as the soil is not malnourished, there is no need to add fertilizer.

"Summer adzuki" is commonly planted around late April to late May in colder areas. "Fall adzuki" is planted around early-to-mid July in neutral or warmer areas. For intercropping of corn, there's a method by which edamame is planted in spring and adzuki beans in fall. The pairing of corn and adzuki is a similar intercropping method.

As corn and adzuki beans have different types of pests that generally avoid each other, this combination can greatly reduce the damage caused by the pests.

**Application** As mentioned above, edamame can be planted in place of adzuki beans (see p. 42).

### CULTIVATION PROCESS

**Selecting varieties** For corn, any sweetcorn variety will work. Use spring-planted adzuki if your corn is an early variety, and summer-planted adzuki if it is a later variety.

**Preparing seedlings** Plant three corn seeds per plastic pot, and pluck out the sprouts once a seedling has 2–3 leaves, to ensure just one plant per pot. Grow it until the plant has four leaves. It takes about 3–4 weeks to have a ground-ready seedling.

**Mixing soil** Three weeks before planting, add fully matured compost and fermented organic fertilizer to prepare.

**Planting, seeding** Plant spring-planted corn in late April to early May. At the same time, plant three adzuki beans per spot. If you are growing corn in fall, plant adzuki bean seeds beforehand in early-to-mid July. Corn will then be planted in mid-August to early September.

**Adding fertilizer** Usually not necessary. If the soil is poor, you can add a handful of fertilizer every three weeks. Adzuki tends to overgrow the vines when there is too much nutrient in the soil.

**Earthing up** Once corn develops lateral roots near the base, earth up. Adzuki also grows better if you earth up the adzuki several times.

**Harvesting** The harvest period for corn is 60–70 days after planting. If you planted spring-planted adzuki, harvest it in mid-July to early August. For summer-planted adzuki, harvest it in early October to mid-November when the leaves start dying and the pod starts developing.

### TIP

Adzuki requires 120–140 days for cultivation. Start cultivation at the right time; make sure not to miss the window for planting.

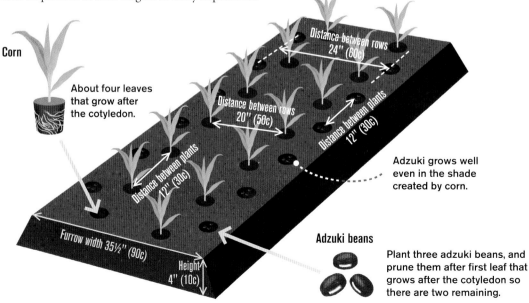

**Corn**

About four leaves that grow after the cotyledon.

Distance between rows 24" (60c)

Distance between rows 20" (50c)

Distance between plants 12" (30c)

Distance between plants 12" (30c)

Furrow width 35½" (90c)

Height 4" (10c)

Adzuki grows well even in the shade created by corn.

**Adzuki beans**

Plant three adzuki beans, and prune them after first leaf that grows after the cotyledon so there are two remaining.

# Corn & Taro

Speeds up growth

Efficient use of space

## Taro grows in the shade during the summer, corn grows well during fall

Corn is not limited as to how much it can grow according to the level of sunlight it gets. Therefore, the more sunlight it gets the better corn grows. By contrast, taro does not like strong light in summer, so the growth slows down. It is better when taro grows in a place where there's some shade. This pairing allows taro to grow in the shade of the corn plant.

Corn planted in spring is harvested by early August, so you can till the furrow to grow corn in fall from late August to early September. Taro has bacteria that enrich the soil, but the effect becomes apparent only in the latter half of the cultivation. During fall, if you plant corn near taro, there's no need to add fertilizer.

### CULTIVATION PROCESS

**Selecting varieties** Any variety can work for both plants.

**Mixing soil** Three weeks before planting, add fully matured compost and fermented organic fertilizer to prepare.

**Planting** Plant corn in late April to late May. Plant taro around late April to mid-May.

**Adding fertilizer** If the soil is poor, add a handful of fermented organic fertilizer every three weeks.

**Earthing up, straw mulch** Earth up the corn once it starts growing lateral roots. For taro, lay down straw mulch after earthing up in early June and in early July. Place straw mulch before the rainy season starts.

**Harvesting** You can harvest corn (sweetcorn) 60–70 days after planting. Harvest taro before it's exposed to frost.

### TIP

If possible, grow corn on a furrow that extends from east to west. Grow taro on the northern side of that furrow. If you are growing corn on a furrow that extends from north to south, plant taro in a place that has the most shade.

---

**Mitsuba (Japanese hornwort) grows well in shade**
You can also grow mitsuba in the shade created by corn. As mitsuba seedlings do not grow big, you can plant them together on the same furrow. As corn grows side roots mitsuba grows straight roots, they will not compete against each other much.

---

You can also grow mitsuba on the corner of the northern furrow.

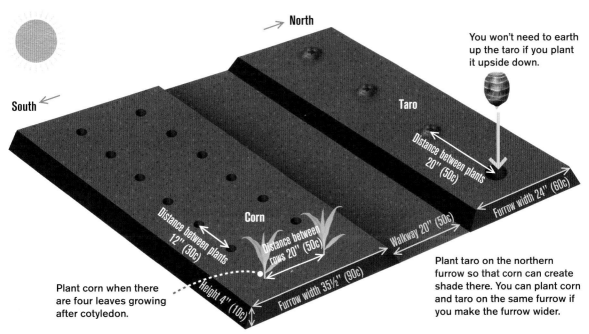

North

You won't need to earth up the taro if you plant it upside down.

South

Taro

Distance between plants 20" (50c)

Furrow width 24" (60c)

Distance between plants 12" (30c)

Corn

Distance between rows 20" (50c)

Walkway 20" (50c)

Height 4" (10c)

Furrow width 35½" (90c)

Plant corn when there are four leaves growing after cotyledon.

Plant taro on the northern furrow so that corn can create shade there. You can plant corn and taro on the same furrow if you make the furrow wider.

# Edamame & Corn

## With this combination, corn grows well without any fertilizer

Edamame roots have root nodule bacteria that capture nitrogen in the atmosphere and enrich the soil. If corn is grown near edamame, the fibrous roots that grow will absorb these nutrients and the plant will grow well. In addition, edamame roots often have mycorrhizal fungus, and so phosphoric acid and other minerals feed the corn. When mycorrhizal fungus exists, it is also known that there will be more root nodule bacteria.

For a home garden, you can either grow edamame between two rows of corn or grow edamame on both sides of the corn. In farms that grow these vegetables on a large scale, several rows of the same plant are grown together for efficiency.

**Application** You can also use adzuki beans instead of edamame (see p. 40).

### CULTIVATION PROCESS

**Selecting varieties** Use a white-bean or brown-bean variety of edamame that grows relatively early. Choose the same variety even if you are planting them in fall. If you plant a black-bean variety of edamame, it will not grow large enough until the end of fall. For corn, any sweetcorn variety will work well.

**Preparing seedlings** Plant three corn seeds per plastic pot, and pluck out the sprouts once a seedling has 2–3 leaves, to ensure just one plant per pot. Grow it until the plant has four leaves. It takes about 3–4 weeks to have a ground-ready seedling.

**Mixing soil** Three weeks before planting, add fully matured compost and fermented organic fertilizer to prepare.

**Planting, seeding** Plant corn in late April to late May. At the same time, plant three edamame seeds per spot, and crop the sprouts at 1½ leaves after the cotyledon. Grow two plants per plastic pot.

**Adding fertilizer** Not necessary.

**Earthing up** Once corn develops lateral roots near the base, earth up. Edamame also grows better if you earth up the edamame several times.

**Harvesting** You can harvest corn 60–70 days after planting, and edamame 80–90 days after planting.

### TIP

You can safely grow edamame if you protect it with nets or nonwoven fabric after it sprouts.

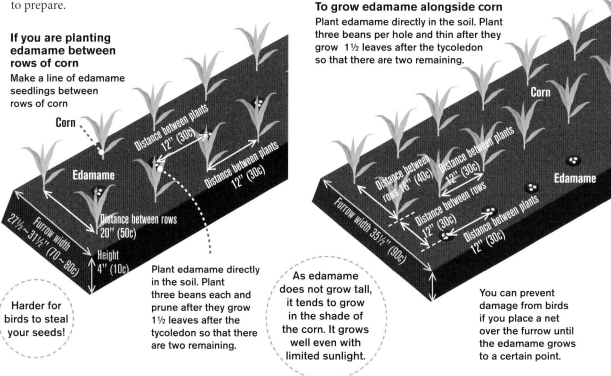

**If you are planting edamame between rows of corn**
Make a line of edamame seedlings between rows of corn

Corn

Edamame

Distance between plants 12" (30c)

Distance between plants 12" (30c)

Distance between rows 20" (50c)

Furrow width 27½"~31½" (70~80c)

Height 4" (10c)

Harder for birds to steal your seeds!

Plant edamame directly in the soil. Plant three beans each and prune after they grow 1½ leaves after the tycoledon so that there are two remaining.

**To grow edamame alongside corn**
Plant edamame directly in the soil. Plant three beans per hole and thin after they grow 1½ leaves after the tycoledon so that there are two remaining.

Corn

Edamame

Distance between rows 16" (40c)

Distance between plants 12" (30c)

Distance between rows

Distance between plants 12" (30c)

Distance between plants 12" (30c)

Furrow width 35½" (90c)

As edamame does not grow tall, it tends to grow in the shade of the corn. It grows well even with limited sunlight.

You can prevent damage from birds if you place a net over the furrow until the edamame grows to a certain point.

# Let's look at the effects

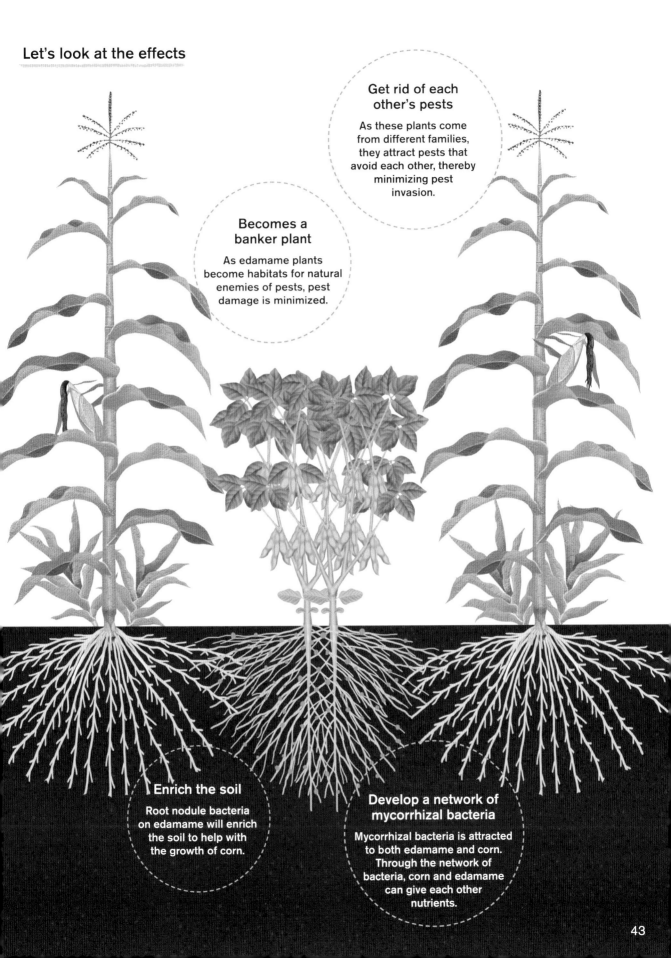

**Get rid of each other's pests**

As these plants come from different families, they attract pests that avoid each other, thereby minimizing pest invasion.

**Becomes a banker plant**

As edamame plants become habitats for natural enemies of pests, pest damage is minimized.

**Enrich the soil**

Root nodule bacteria on edamame will enrich the soil to help with the growth of corn.

**Develop a network of mycorrhizal bacteria**

Mycorrhizal bacteria is attracted to both edamame and corn. Through the network of bacteria, corn and edamame can give each other nutrients.

# Edamame & Red Leaf Lettuce

Repels pests   Speeds up growth

## Enhance the growth of edamame by covering up the ground with leaves and hydrating the furrow

Edamame is grown with a lot of vegetables through companion planting or intercropping methods. As for green vegetables, almost all of them work well with edamame, examples of which are komatsuna (Japanese mustard spinach) and spinach. The root nodule bacteria on edamame roots serve to enrich the soil, vegetables that are paired with it grow well.

It is recommended to grow red leaf lettuce in-between the edamame seedlings or on the corner of the furrow. They grow well even when there is some shade. Red leaf lettuce is an Asteraceae plant and repels pests that are attracted to edamame.

In order to increase the size of harvest for edamame, it is important to never to allow the soil to be dry during the flowering period. Red leaf lettuce keeps moisture in by creating ground cover.

**Application** Instead of edamame, you can also use vineless green beans.

### CULTIVATION PROCESS

**Selecting varieties** Any type of edamame will work. You can expect better pest-repelling results if you choose one of the more vibrant red leaf lettuce varieties.

**Mixing soil** Prepare a furrow three weeks before planting. If the soil is poor, you can add fully matured compost and chaff charcoal when planting.

**Seeding, planting** See p. 45 for edamame. For red leaf lettuce, scatter wet seeds and very thinly cover them with soil. It takes about three weeks to prepare seedlings. Plant red leaf seedlings at the same time as or soon after planting edamame. The same applies when you are growing edamame from seed.

**Adding fertilizer** Not necessary

**Earthing up** Edamame grows well when you earth up a few times.

**Harvesting** Harvest edamame once the beans the pods are enlarged. You can pick and harvest the outer leaves of red leaf lettuce. You can also harvest red leaf lettuce as a whole.

### TIP

It takes about 80 days to grow edamame from seeds to harvest. Red leaf lettuce can be harvested 30–40 days after planting seedlings. As the effect of companion planting is greater in the latter half of cultivation, you can plant red leaf lettuce just before you earth up the edamame.

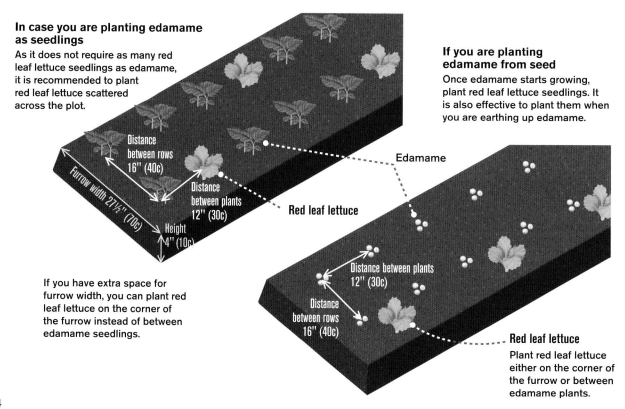

**In case you are planting edamame as seedlings**
As it does not require as many red leaf lettuce seedlings as edamame, it is recommended to plant red leaf lettuce scattered across the plot.

Distance between rows 16" (40c)

Distance between plants 12" (30c)

Furrow width 27½" (70c)

Height 4" (10c)

If you have extra space for furrow width, you can plant red leaf lettuce on the corner of the furrow instead of between edamame seedlings.

**If you are planting edamame from seed**
Once edamame starts growing, plant red leaf lettuce seedlings. It is also effective to plant them when you are earthing up edamame.

Edamame

Red leaf lettuce

Distance between plants 12" (30c)

Distance between rows 16" (40c)

**Red leaf lettuce**
Plant red leaf lettuce either on the corner of the furrow or between edamame plants.

# Edamame & Mint

## Repel stink bugs by using the unique scent of mint

A common pest attracted to edamame is a type of stink bug called *riptortus clavatus*. These bugs absorb liquids from the pea pods, and damage the edamame beans inside or prevent beans from developing. As they tend to grow in number as the temperature rises, the damage is the most severe in summer when beans taste the best.

If you grow mint near edamame, it repels stink bugs. The effect is so good that you'll want to grow this in the same furrow as per companion planting or intercropping; however, mint is a perennial plant and will keep growing if some parts of the roots are still alive under the ground. As it is hard to control once it is planted, it is highly recommended to plant mint in a pot and place it near edamame. If you wish to grow mint on the furrow, growing the plants to frame the plot will function as pest repellent. **Application** Instead of edamame, you can also use Fabaceae plants that suffer from stink bugs such as vineless green beans, cowpea and adzuki beans.

### CULTIVATION PROCESS

**Selecting varieties** Edamame can be any variety. It is recommended to grow strong-scented mint such as peppermint or pennyroyal mint.

**Mixing soil** If the soil is poor, prepare a furrow three weeks before planting by adding matured compost and fermented organic fertilizer.

**Seeding, planting** If you are planting edamame from seed, plant three seeds per hole and thin later to grow two plants per spot. If you are preparing seedlings, plant three seeds per plastic pot, and thin until there are two plants per pot. Seedlings will be ground-ready in three weeks. You can plant store-bought mint seedling in a pot. If you plant mint seeds in mid-to-late March, you can also grow your own mint from scratch.

**Adding fertilizer** Not necessary. Mint that has been grown since the previous year lacks nutrients in the soil—add fertilizer when needed.

**Earthing up** Edamame grows well when you earth up a few times.

**Harvesting** Harvest edamame once it enlarges the beans the pods. The time of harvest depends on the variety. You can pick the mint leaves as they grow.

### TIP

Plant mint in a separate pot, and put the pot slightly underground. This way, the soil can be kept hydrated, eliminating the need for frequent watering. After edamame is harvested, the pot can be moved elsewhere. Mint dies back in winter, but returns in spring.

## Let's look at the effects

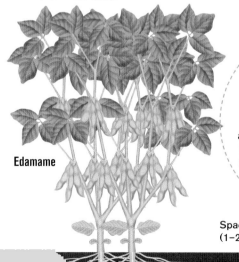

**Edamame**

**Pick the mint to enjoy in tea and so on**

Once the stems start growing, you can frequently pick and use it. Picking the leaves induces the growth and also strengthens the scent. Then, you can expect better pest repellent results.

**Repel pests with the scent of mint**

This can minimize damage from stink bugs and border moths.

**Mint**

Space mint pots every 1–2 yards (1–2 m) on the edamame furrow

It helps to plant mint in

Place the pot halfway

# Vine Type Green Beans & Arugula

Efficient use of space  Repels pests  Speeds up growth

## You can harvest aromatic herbs as a companion for green beans

Vine type green beans will grow upwards, attaching their vines to the nets or trellis. This companion planting method will use the empty space around the base to grow one more type of plant. Arugula is a Brassicaceae family plant and is a favorite in salads. As it is tough, it will grow healthily at the foot of the green bean plants.

Due to the root nodule bacteria on green bean roots, the soil is enriched and the arugula will grow well. On the other hand, arugula covers the ground near green bean roots and functions as mulch, which moisturizes the soil and prevents weeds. The scent also acts as a pest repellent. Arugula can be planted around early March to late October, so you can plant arugula again after the first batch has been harvested. You can also plant arugula seeds when you plant green beans in fall.

**Application** Arugula can be planted near peas and can be mix cultivated.

### CULTIVATION PROCESS

**Selecting varieties** There are many types of green beans. It is easier to grow a variety local to you. Arugula comes in a variety of flavor intensities, so choose your favorite.

**Mixing soil** Prepare a furrow three weeks before planting seeds. If the soil is rich, fertilizers are unnecessary. If the soil is poor, add mature compost when planting.

**Seeding** Plant three green beans per spot. Crop the sprouts after leaf that grows after the cotyledon so there are 1–2 plants per spot. Plant arugula from seeds as well.

**Adding fertilizer** Not necessary.

**Harvesting** You can harvest green beans for a longer period if you start harvesting them earlier. If you allow beans to grow large, the plant starts aging and dies sooner. Harvest arugula from the outer leaves once the number of leaves has increased.

### TIP

This combination can easily be recreated in planter pots. You can grow a green curtain using green bean vines, and grow arugula in the free space.

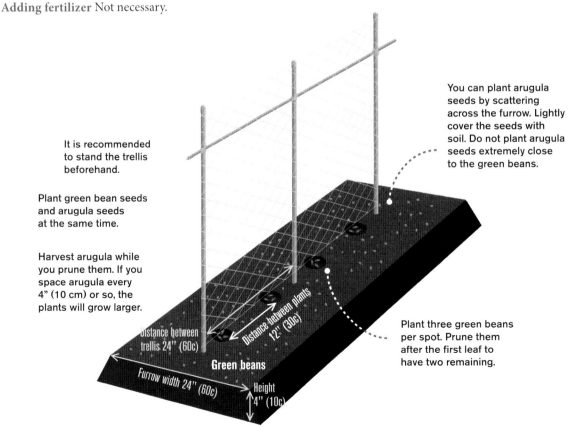

You can plant arugula seeds by scattering across the furrow. Lightly cover the seeds with soil. Do not plant arugula seeds extremely close to the green beans.

It is recommended to stand the trellis beforehand.

Plant green bean seeds and arugula seeds at the same time.

Harvest arugula while you prune them. If you space arugula every 4" (10 cm) or so, the plants will grow larger.

Distance between plants 12" (30c)

Distance between trellis 24" (60c)

Green beans

Furrow width 24" (60c)

Height 4" (10c)

Plant three green beans per spot. Prune them after the first leaf to have two remaining.

# Vine Type Green Beans & Bitter Melon

Efficient use of space   Repels pests   Speeds up growth

## Maximize your net or trellis. These plants also make a nice green curtain in your window

By combining vine type green beans and bitter melon, which also grows vines, you can maximize the net or trellis. Green bean plant is a Fabaceae plant, so it has root nodule bacteria that capture the nitrogen in the air and enrich the soil nearby. Bitter melon grows well because it uses the nutrients created by the bacteria. Bitter melon is a Cucurbitaceae plant, and as it has a unique scent, it rarely has any pests. Therefore, green beans also have fewer pests. You can also grow these plants in planters and pots to use as green curtains in the window sills and verandas.

**Application** You can also use cowpea (the kind with vines) and winged beans instead of green beans. Instead of bitter melon, you can also use sponge cucumber, cucumber and oriental melon as alternatives.

## CULTIVATION PROCESS

**Selecting varieties** Both plants can be any variety.

**Mixing soil** Prepare a furrow three weeks before planting seeds. If the soil is poor, add mature compost.

**Seeding, planting** Plant two bitter melon seeds per plastic pot. Pluck out one sprout to grow one plant per pot when it grows two leaves. You can plant the seedling when there are 3–4 leaves, and plant green bean seeds at the same time. You should plant three green bean seeds per spot, and crop the sprouts once it grows the leaf and a half that grows after cotyledon. Immediately after planting the plants until the sprouts are cropped, cover the soil with net or cheesecloth to prevent bird damage.

**Adding fertilizer** Not necessary

**Harvesting** Harvest beans before they harden. Harvest bitter melon as the fruits grow large enough.

## TIP

Both Cucurbitae plants and Fabaceae plants can suffer from root rot nematode. Therefore, do not try this combination if root rot nematode tends to be a problem in your garden.

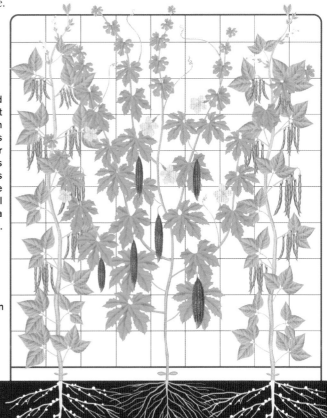

Stand the trellis and guide nets from the start of cultivation. Green beans will grow vines almost perpendicular to the ground, whereas bitter melon grows its vines diagonally. The vines will integrate well together to create a beautiful green curtain.

Plant three green beans per 1 spot. Prune them after the first leaf to have two remaining

Distance between plants 8~12" (20~30c)

Plant bitter melon when it has 3–4 leaves after the cotyledon. Do not plant them too deep.

# Cabbage & Red Leaf Lettuce

## Prevent damage sustained by pests like budworm using the unique scent of lettuce

When thinking of pests attracted to cabbage, you may immediately think of caterpillars. Mixing Brassicaceae plant with Asteraceae plants can help repel cabbage butterflies and cabbage moths. Although you can also use iceberg lettuce, since cabbage butterflies and cabbage moths have an aversion to the color red, this combination is more effective. Cabbage is also useful for repelling pests such as plant lice that are attracted to red leaf lettuce.

If you are planting in spring, you can plant both at once. If you are planting in fall, it is recommended to grow red leaf lettuce large enough to repel budworms in September to October when the damage is most prevalent.

**Application** In place of cabbage, you can plant broccoli and cauliflower. Combining a Brassicaceae plant with an Asteraceae plant will have the same pest-repelling effect.

### CULTIVATION PROCESS

**Selecting varieties** Any variety can work for cabbage. It is recommended to choose red leaf lettuce over other types of leaf lettuce. If you use this combination in fall, red leaf lettuce can be planted first to prepare seedlings.

**Mixing soil** Three weeks before planting, add fully matured compost and fermented organic fertilizer to prepare.

**Planting** If planting in spring, you can plant in mid-to-late April. If you are planting in fall, plant by early September to early October. If you would like to harvest the plants in spring, you can plant them in late October. In these later months, however, cabbage isn't so vulnerable to pests as to make this pairing worthwhile.

**Earthing up, adding fertilizer** three weeks after planting cabbage, add a handful of fermented organic fertilizer and earth up. Once cabbage starts growing heads, add another handful of fertilizer.

**Harvesting** Harvest cabbage heads if the top of the head feels firm when pressed. Harvest red leaf lettuce by either picking the outer leaves or cutting the whole plant.

### TIP

If you are planting red leaf lettuce in spring, keep growing the plant by harvesting the outer leaves. If you are planting in fall, you can harvest the whole plant once the temperature drops and there's no pest damage.

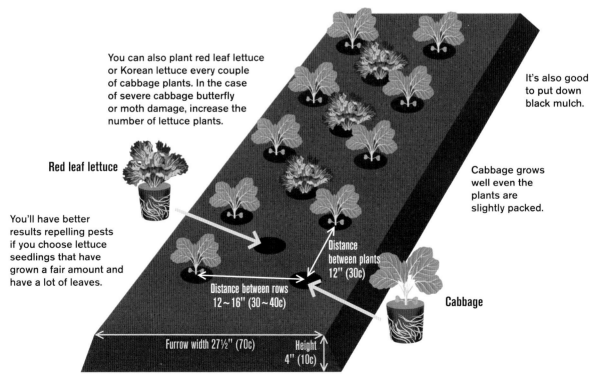

You can also plant red leaf lettuce or Korean lettuce every couple of cabbage plants. In the case of severe cabbage butterfly or moth damage, increase the number of lettuce plants.

It's also good to put down black mulch.

Red leaf lettuce

You'll have better results repelling pests if you choose lettuce seedlings that have grown a fair amount and have a lot of leaves.

Cabbage grows well even the plants are slightly packed.

Distance between plants 12" (30c)

Distance between rows 12~16" (30~40c)

Furrow width 27½" (70c)

Height 4" (10c)

Cabbage

# Let's look at the effects

## Repel each other's pests

The species of plant lice that are attracted to Brassicaceae plants and Asteraceae plants differ, "canceling out" plant lice on both plants.

### Salvia is also effective for repelling pests

To make use of the cabbage butterfly's and moth's aversion to red, you can also grow red-flowered salvia with cabbage or broccoli. Though there are many varieties of salvia available, *salvia splendens* is particularly efficient. It grows well in the heat of summer when pests are most prevalent

## Prevent budworms

Cabbage butterflies and moths will not be attracted to the cabbage, as they dislike the smell of Asteraceae plants such as red leaf lettuce.

Cabbage butterflies and moths tend to dislike the color red.

## Both grow well together

Cabbage is a mutual prosperity type of plant, which coexist with other vegetables growing nearby.

# Cabbage & Fava Beans

Speeds up growth

Repels pests

Efficient use of space

## Use cabbage to shield fava beans from cold wind. Let these plants enhance each other's growth

A common mistake when growing fava beans is allowing them to be exposed to cold, wind or frost before they have proper root growth after being planted in fall. There is a way to shield fava beans from cold wind by using windbreak nets or bamboo with leaves, but if you plant cabbage or broccoli you can protect fava beans from the cold and allow them to grow healthy roots. This is especially effective when fava bean cultivation has a late start.

Plant fava bean seedlings in-between cabbages in early November to early December. Fava beans will grow roots well if you cut the tips of the roots before planting. Next spring, as fava bean roots have root nodule bacteria that enrich the nearby soil, cabbage will also grow well. Also, while fava beans tend to have plant lice, they will also attract ladybugs, which will kill the plant lice on both beans and cabbage. **Application** In place of cabbage, you can also use broccoli, cauliflower, and kale. Peas make a good alternative to fava beans.

## CULTIVATION PROCESS

**Selecting varieties** Choose a type of cabbage that is planted in fall and harvested in spring. Any fava bean variety will work.

**Mixing soil** Three weeks before planting, add fully matured compost and fermented organic fertilizer to prepare.

**Planting, seeding** Plant cabbage in late October to early November if it is a fall-planted, spring-harvested variety. Plant fava bean seeds in the latter half of October to prepare seedlings. Plant the seedlings between the cabbage rows in early November to early December.

**Earthing up** About three weeks after planting cabbage, earth up.

**Harvesting** Harvest cabbage heads if the top of the head feels firm when pressed. Harvest fava beans in the latter half of May. It is good to harvest when the bean pod faces downwards and the ridge starts to brown.

## TIP

Cabbage that is planted in the latter half of September serves as a shield from the cold wind. If you leave five outer leaves behind when harvesting, these leaves will protect fava beans from wind, and the leaves will help the soil retain moisture. In spring, the leaves left behind will develop sprouts. You can harvest 2–3 cabbage heads about the size of your fist.

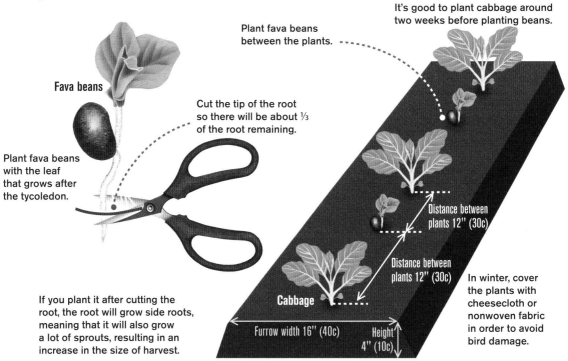

It's good to plant cabbage around two weeks before planting beans.

Plant fava beans between the plants.

Fava beans

Cut the tip of the root so there will be about ⅓ of the root remaining.

Plant fava beans with the leaf that grows after the tycoledon.

Distance between plants 12" (30c)

Distance between plants 12" (30c)

Cabbage

In winter, cover the plants with cheesecloth or nonwoven fabric in order to avoid bird damage.

If you plant it after cutting the root, the root will grow side roots, meaning that it will also grow a lot of sprouts, resulting in an increase in the size of harvest.

Furrow width 16" (40c)

Height 4" (10c)

# Cabbage & Chickweed, Clover

Speeds up growth    Repels pests

## Natural mulch helps with the growth of cabbage between fall and early summer

Cabbage is a great match with vegetables and weeds that grow close to it—you can call cabbage a co-prosperity type plant. In contrast, you may call Chinese cabbage, also a Brassicaceae plant, a destructionist type plant—vegetables or weeds do not grow well around Chinese cabbage.

Chickweed is a weed that grows on farms during fall to spring. The soil where it grows is very rich, so cabbage of course grows well there.

Chickweed sprouts suddenly in late October, and will cover the furrows and walkways, so you can leave it as it is. As the soil does not get direct wind exposure, it stays hydrated and cabbage grows well. As the plot is also being used during winter, microorganisms remain active, and thus the soil quality will be kept enriched.

In the case of cabbage that is planted in spring and harvested in summer, clover can be used. As clover also covers the surface of the ground, it functions as mulch. Additionally, as it is a Fabaceae plant, it will enrich the soil. Beneficial insects will be attracted to clover, helping reduce pest damage to cabbage.

**Application** As an alternative to cabbage, you can use broccoli, green pak choi or tatsoi.

### CULTIVATION PROCESS

**Selecting varieties** Choose varieties that will not get bushy. If you are planting to harvest in summer or winter, you can grow most varieties. You can buy clover seeds in stores or online.

**Mixing soil** Three weeks before planting, add fully matured compost and fermented organic fertilizer to prepare. If you are planting clover, plant the clover seeds after preparing a furrow in November.

**Planting** Plant cabbage seedlings when they have 4–5 leaves. It is common space plants at 20" (50 cm), but you can also grow smaller cabbage by planting them every 12" (30 cm).

**Adding fertilizer, earthing up** Three weeks after planting cabbage, add a handful of fermented organic fertilizer and earth up. Once cabbage starts growing heads, add another handful of fertilizer.

**Harvesting** Harvest cabbage heads if the top of the head feels firm when pressed.

### TIP

When chickweed and clover start getting tall, cut them short so cabbage receives enough sunlight. White clover, once established, regenerates from the roots even if weeded, and it becomes difficult to manage, so limit the space where you grow it.

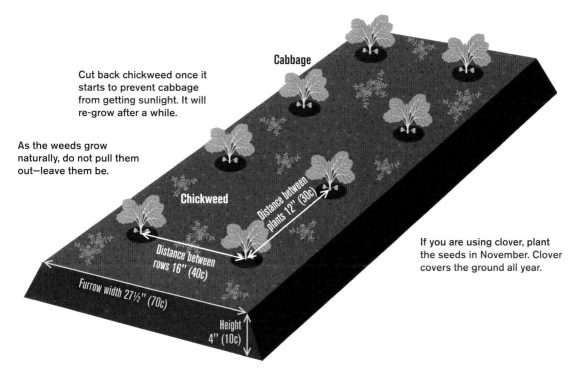

Cabbage

Cut back chickweed once it starts to prevent cabbage from getting sunlight. It will re-grow after a while.

As the weeds grow naturally, do not pull them out—leave them be.

Chickweed

Distance between plants 12" (30c)

Distance between rows 16" (40c)

Furrow width 27½" (70c)

Height 4" (10c)

If you are using clover, plant the seeds in November. Clover covers the ground all year.

# Chinese Cabbage & Oats

Prevents disease   Speeds up growth   Repels pests

## Prevent clubroot by utilizing oat roots' bacteria

Chinese cabbage grows big outer leaves, and the number of leaves increases as it grows. By the end of fall, you can harvest a big, heavy Chinese cabbage with thick leaves. However, if Chinese cabbage sustains damage from pests or clubroots during its growth stage, it will enter winter before it has enough leaves to shape itself.

Mixed planting of oats can prevent clubroots. Oats produce an antibiotic substance called saponin that prevents soil-borne diseases. When oats are grown near Chinese cabbage, this substance reduces the density of bacteria that cause clubroots. This ensures that Chinese cabbage grows well. In addition, oats will become a habitat for beneficial insects that kill the pests on the Chinese cabbage.

**Application** You can also use cabbage, Japanese mustard spinach or turnip instead of Chinese cabbage.

### CULTIVATION PROCESS

**Selecting varieties** Any variety can work for Chinese cabbage. Oat is considered to be more effective for disease prevention if it is naturally grown, but commercial green manure can also be used.

**Mixing soil** Three weeks before planting, add fully matured compost and fermented organic fertilizer to prepare.

**Seeding, planting** Plant Chinese cabbage seeds in plastic pots by the end of August to raise seedlings. Plant seedlings from mid to late September. Oats may be planted at the same time as Chinese cabbage, or it may be effective to plant it from late August to early September, immediately after preparing a furrow.

**Adding fertilizer** Since you want to the outer leaves to grow large, fertilize the soil on one side of the walkway three weeks after planting. Two weeks after that, put fertilizer on the other side and earth up. In another three weeks, fertilize the four corners of the furrow. Each time, add a handful of fermented organic fertilizer.

**Harvesting** Harvest Chinese cabbage if the top of the head feels firm when pressed.

### TIP

When the oat plants become tall, cut them short so the cabbage receives enough sunlight. You can use the cut leaves and stems as mulch.

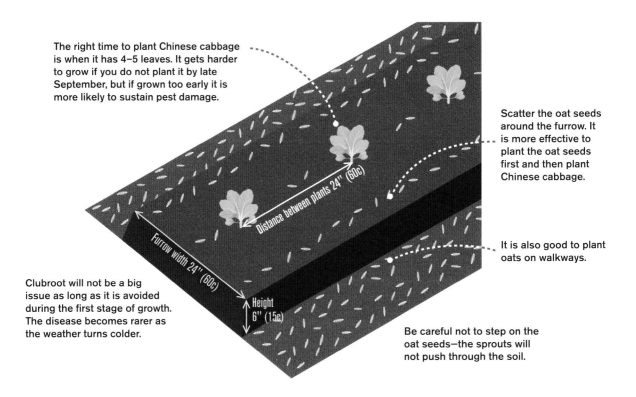

The right time to plant Chinese cabbage is when it has 4–5 leaves. It gets harder to grow if you do not plant it by late September, but if grown too early it is more likely to sustain pest damage.

Distance between plants 24" (60c)

Furrow width 24" (60c)

Height 6" (15c)

Scatter the oat seeds around the furrow. It is more effective to plant the oat seeds first and then plant Chinese cabbage.

It is also good to plant oats on walkways.

Clubroot will not be a big issue as long as it is avoided during the first stage of growth. The disease becomes rarer as the weather turns colder.

Be careful not to step on the oat seeds—the sprouts will not push through the soil.

# Chinese Cabbage & Nasturtium

Repels pests

## Nasturtium increases the number of beneficial insects and prevents pest damage on Chinese cabbage

Nasturtium is an annual plant that belongs to the Tropaeolaceae family. The flowers and leaves have slight spiciness and sourness, and can be used in salads, or cooked. If you plant nasturtium with a Brassicaceae plant like Chinese cabbage, its scent can repel plant lice. Also, nasturtium can work as a banker plant as leaves and stems attract spider mites and thrips, but will also attract beneficial insects.

As nasturtium does not like high temperatures or high humidity in summer, it is best to either let it survive the summer in a place where westering sun will not affect it, or to grow the seedlings late August to early September. You can plant one nasturtium seedling per 3–4 Chinese cabbage seedlings.

**Application** Nasturtium works for Brassicaceae plants such as cabbage, broccoli, komatsuna (Japanese mustard spinach) and turnip. It also works well with Solanaceae plants like eggplants and green peppers, and Asteraceae plants like lettuce.

### CULTIVATION PROCESS

**Selecting varieties** Any variety can work for Chinese cabbage. Nasturtium seedlings and seeds are available in garden centers.

**Mixing soil** Three weeks before planting, add fully matured compost and fermented organic fertilizer to prepare.

**Seeding, planting** Plant Chinese cabbage seeds in plastic pots by the end of August to raise seedlings. Plant seedlings is from mid to late September. If you are growing nasturtium from seeds, plant them in late August to early September. You can plant the seedling once it has 3–4 leaves.

**Adding fertilizer** See p. 52

**Harvesting** For Chinese cabbage, see p. 52. For nasturtium, harvest flowers and leaves whenever necessary to use them for salads, etc. The seeds can be pickled.

### TIP

Nasturtium spreads sideways, but can be left alone unless it covers the leaves of Chinese cabbage. It begins to die at the end of fall and is almost finished when the Chinese cabbage heads up. It may sprout from the spilled seeds in the next spring.

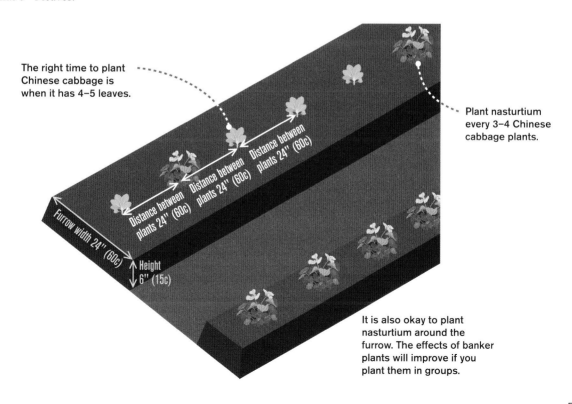

The right time to plant Chinese cabbage is when it has 4–5 leaves.

Distance between plants 24" (60c)

Distance between plants 24" (60c)

Distance between plants 24" (60c)

Furrow width 24" (60c)

Height 6" (15c)

Plant nasturtium every 3–4 Chinese cabbage plants.

It is also okay to plant nasturtium around the furrow. The effects of banker plants will improve if you plant them in groups.

# Japanese Mustard Spinach & Green Leaf Lettuce

Repels pests

## Never allow budworms or plant lice to stay on your plant!

Both Japanese mustard spinach (komatsuna) and green leaf lettuce have a relatively short cultivation period, and they can be grown in the same furrow. Japanese mustard spinach is a Brassicaceae plant, and often suffers from pests such as budworms and plant lice. When you plant an Asteraceae plant such as green leaf lettuce, you can effectively eliminate pests.

You can observe the same effect when you use green pak choi, turnip or potherb mustard in place of Japanese mustard spinach. Though it is common to grow these plants together in one spot between spring and fall, it is recommended to grow green leaf lettuce or other green vegetables between the rows of these plants.

**Application** You can also plant crown daisy instead of green leaf lettuce.

### CULTIVATION PROCESS

**Selecting varieties** Any variety can work for Japanese mustard spinach. Interspersing red leaf lettuce among green leaf lettuce can maximize the pest repelling effects.

**Mixing soil** Three weeks before planting, add fully matured compost and fermented organic fertilizer to prepare.

**Seeding** Plant Japanese mustard spinach seeds directly in the soil. You can plant them early April to late May in spring, or late August to early October in fall. You can either plant green leaf lettuce directly as seeds, or prepare seedlings first. You can plant the seeds from late March to early October, except for mid-July to mid-August.

**Thinning** Crop the plants when Japanese mustard spinach has 1–2 leaves after the cotyledon, to grow the plant every 1–1½" (3–4 cm). Once the plant reaches app. 3" (7–8 cm) in height, space the plants at 2–3" (5–7 cm).

If you plant green leaf lettuce seeds directly in the soil, thin the plants so that the leaves slightly overlap with the plants next to them. In the end, grow plants every 6" (15 cm). You can use the thinned plants as well.

**Adding fertilizer** If the soil is poor and the Japanese mustard spinach leaves start yellowing, add fermented organic fertilizer between the rows of plants or on the corner of the furrow. Lightly mix the fertilizer into the soil.

**Harvesting** You can harvest Japanese mustard spinach in 40–60 days. Harvest once it grows large enough. You can harvest green leaf lettuce by either cutting the outer leaves or picking the whole plant.

### TIP

Because the damage to pests is more severe at high temperatures, it is better to plant the green leaf lettuce seedlings first when growing them in fall to increase pest control effects.

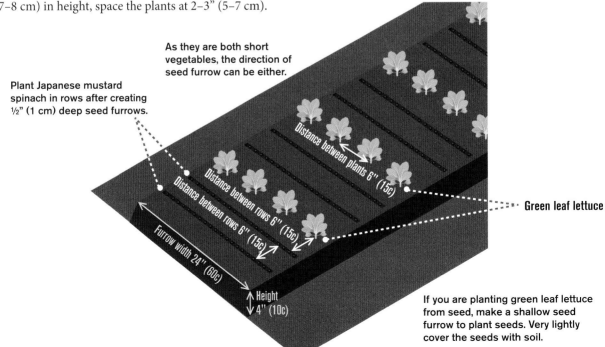

As they are both short vegetables, the direction of seed furrow can be either.

Plant Japanese mustard spinach in rows after creating ½" (1 cm) deep seed furrows.

Distance between plants 6" (15c)

Distance between rows 6" (15c)

Furrow width 24" (60c)

Height 4" (10c)

Green leaf lettuce

If you are planting green leaf lettuce from seed, make a shallow seed furrow to plant seeds. Very lightly cover the seeds with soil.

# Japanese Mustard Spinach & Garlic Chives

## Protect Japanese mustard spinach from damage by leaf beetles

Japanese mustard spinach (komatsuna) that is planted in fall sometimes gets small holes everywhere on the leaves, occasionally reaching the point at which the leaves look like lace. If you find a black insect about ¹⁄₁₆" (4 mm) in size on the leaves, it's probably a pest called leaf beetle. It falls from the leaf easily and escapes quickly, so leaf beetles are a common problem to all Brassicaceae family plants.

As leaf beetles hate the scent of garlic chives, it's good to grow garlic chives in the same furrow or on a furrow nearby. It is recommended to constantly harvest garlic chives as they grow, so that the liquid released from the garlic chive leaves' scars will continually repel leaf beetles. It is even effective to place cut garlic chive leaves on the furrow where Japanese mustard spinach is growing.

**Application** You can expect the same effect of garlic chives on other Brassicaceae plants such as cabbage, broccoli, Chinese cabbage, green pak choi, potherb mustard, turnip, and daikon.

## CULTIVATION PROCESS

**Selecting varieties** Any variety will work for both plants.

**Mixing soil** Three weeks before planting, add fully matured compost and fermented organic fertilizer to prepare.

**Seeding, planting** Plant Japanese mustard spinach seeds directly in the soil. You can plant them from late August to early October. Chives can be planted from store-bought seedlings, or you can plant seeds in late March to raise seedlings. Plant the seedlings in June. Garlic chives grow well when three of them are planted in one spot.

**Adding fertilizer** See p. 54.

**Harvesting** For Japanese mustard spinach, see p. 54. Keep chives trimmed to about 1½" (3 cm) above ground.

## TIP

Leaf beetles are mainly fall pests. Once Japanese mustard spinach sprouts push through, cut garlic chives to about 1½" (3 cm) away from the bottom of the stock, and place the cuttings in-between the rows of Japanese mustard spinach. In addition to pest control, this helps garlic chive grow soft and fragrant leaves.

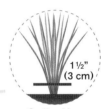

Once garlic chives grow tall, trim them and lay the cuttings down. The scent from freshly-cut leaves is especially effective for repelling pests.

1½" (3 cm)

**Garlic chives**

You can either plant garlic chives in the way that you plant green leaf lettuce (p. 54), or plant it near the Japanese mustard spinach furrow, on the walkways and so on. Either way, it is effective to lay down cut garlic chive leaves between the rows of Japanese mustard spinach.

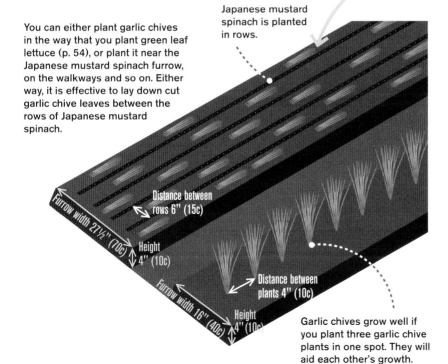

Japanese mustard spinach is planted in rows.

Distance between rows 6" (15c)

Furrow width 27½" (70c)

Height 4" (10c)

Furrow width 16" (40c)

Distance between plants 4" (10c)

Height 4" (10c)

Garlic chives grow well if you plant three garlic chive plants in one spot. They will aid each other's growth.

**Mulch cultivation of goosefoot and lambsquarters**

You can also grow Japanese mustard spinach and similar using goosefoot or lambsquarters, which can repel pests that are attracted to Brassicaceae plants, serve as mulch to keep the soil hydrated, and prevent weeds from growing. Trim plants down once they block sunlight to your mustard spinach These are annuals and will die at the end of fall.

# Spinach & Green Onion

Speeds up growth    Prevents disease

## Grow healthy and delicious spinach using this method

Fusarium wilt is a soil-borne disease that is a common problem to spinach and can kill the plant. The microorganisms on the green onion roots release antibiotic bacteria and eliminate the bacteria that causes fusarium wilt.

Also, green onion is a monocotyledonous plant that likes to absorb ammonia nitrogen. On the other hand, spinach is a dicotyledonous plant that likes nitrate nitrogen, which is made by breaking down ammonia nitrogen.

The reason spinach leaves sometimes taste bitter is because the plant absorbed too much nitrate nitrogen. Green onion absorbs the excess nutrients, giving spinach a fresh taste.

**Application** You can also use shallot or Asatsuki (Japanese chives) instead of green onion. It is difficult to earth up the furrow if you plant scallions with spinach.

### CULTIVATION PROCESS

**Selecting varieties** If you are planting spinach in spring, choose a type that won't easily become bushy. For green onion, any variety will work.

**Mixing soil** Three weeks before planting, add fully matured compost and fermented organic fertilizer to prepare.

**Seeding, planting** Spinach can be planted from spring to fall, except for midsummer. Spinach is planted in rows. Plant green onion at the same time. The appropriate time for planting green onion seeds is March and September. It takes 30 days or more to raise seedlings.

**Thinning, adding fertilizer** Spinach is thinned to 1–1½" (3–4 cm). between plants with a single leaf after the cotyledon, and again at 2½–3" (6–8 cm). between plants with a plant height of 2–2½" (5–6 cm). At the time of thinning for the second time, add fermented organic fertilizer to both spinach and green onion.

**Harvesting** Spinach can be harvested at a plant height of about 10" (25 cm). Green onion leaves will grow again if the leaves are harvested leaving about 1½" (3 cm) of stock.

### TIP

Spinach is difficult to grow in acidic soils of pH 6 or less. If necessary, add lime (e.g. shellfish lime and magnesia lime) and adjust the acidity to approach neutrality (pH 7). Green onion grows well in the same environment.

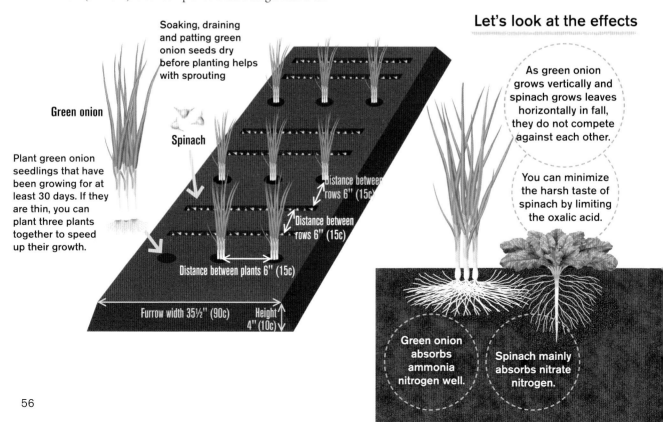

Soaking, draining and patting green onion seeds dry before planting helps with sprouting

Green onion

Spinach

Plant green onion seedlings that have been growing for at least 30 days. If they are thin, you can plant three plants together to speed up their growth.

Distance between rows 6" (15c)

Distance between rows 6" (15c)

Distance between plants 6" (15c)

Furrow width 35½" (90c)    Height 4" (10c)

### Let's look at the effects

As green onion grows vertically and spinach grows leaves horizontally in fall, they do not compete against each other.

You can minimize the harsh taste of spinach by limiting the oxalic acid.

Green onion absorbs ammonia nitrogen well.

Spinach mainly absorbs nitrate nitrogen.

# Spinach & Greater Burdock

## Combine straight-rooted vegetables to grow deeper roots

Greater burdock grows long stems and big leaves, so it requires an exceptionally wide space. You can grow and harvest spinach on the same furrow while greater burdock is still young and growing. There are varieties whose seeds are planted mid-April to early May and harvested in fall, and others whose seeds are planted mid-September to early October and harvested in spring. The best type to pair with spinach is harvested in spring.

Greater burdock is a straight-and-deep-rooted plant. Till the furrow up to 24–27½" (60–70 cm) deep. Spinach is also a straight-rooted plant, so it grows well on furrows that have been deeply tilled.

### CULTIVATION PROCESS

**Selecting varieties** Any variety will work for both plants.

**Mixing soil** For burdock root, dig up to a depth of 24–27½" (60–70 cm) three weeks before planting seeds to soften the soil. Return the soil and prepare a furrow. Do not apply mature compost or fermented organic fertilizer.

**Seeding** Spring greater burdock is planted from mid-September to early-October. See p. 56 for spinach. Burdock seeds should be soaked for a day before planting. Plant 5–6 grains in one spot and cover with soil.

**Thinning, adding fertilizer** See p. 56 for thinning spinach. Thin greater burdock once it grows one leaf after the cotyledon, and again when it has three leaves. Add fermented organic fertilizer only around the spinach at the second thinning.

**Harvesting** See page 56 for spinach. Harvest burdock from mid-June to early August in the following year.

### TIP

Salad burdock (short roots) can be harvested by the end of August. In this case, plant spinach seeds at the same time, or slightly later.

Till the ground up to 24–27½" (60–70 cm) deep. If growing a salad burdock, it can be about 12" (30 cm) deep.

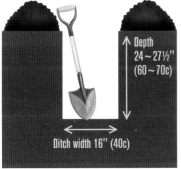

Depth 24 ~ 27½" (60 ~ 70c)

Ditch width 16" (40c)

After returning ⅔ of the soil, tamp it down to harden it. This prevents the furrow from caving in.

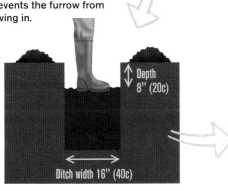

Depth 8" (20c)

Ditch width 16" (40c)

**Greater burdock**
Plant 5–6 seeds per spot. Soak the seeds in water for a day before planting.

**Spinach**
Keep 6" (15 cm) distance from the burdock. Plant spinach seeds in a line, ½" (1 cm) apart.

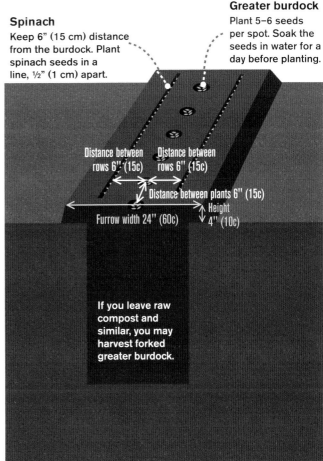

Distance between rows 6" (15c)    Distance between rows 6" (15c)

Distance between plants 6" (15c)

Height 4" (10c)

Furrow width 24" (60c)

If you leave raw compost and similar, you may harvest forked greater burdock.

# Crown Daisy & Green Pak Choi

Repels pests

## Repel pests on green pak choi by using the scent of crown daisy

Similar to the way to grow cabbage and red leaf lettuce (see p. 48), this is pairing of a Brassicaceae plant with an Asteraceae plant. By planting crown daisy nearby, you can prevent cabbage butterflies or cabbage moths from lighting on the green pak choi, which will therefore prevent their laying eggs on the leaves, ultimately preventing worm damage later on.

As these plants prefer different types of nutrients, they improve each other's flavor by controlling the amount each receives. Crown daisy can be sown in the ground in April. As green pak choi is more susceptible to pest damage, it is recommended to grow crown daisy first for better results.

**Application** In place of green pak choi, you can also plant Japanese mustard, potherb mustard or turnips. Green leaf lettuce is a great alternative to crown daisy.

### CULTIVATION PROCESS

**Selecting varieties** For green pak choi, any variety will work. For crown daisy, see p. 61.

**Mixing soil** Three weeks before planting, add fully matured compost and fermented organic fertilizer to prepare.

**Seeding** Plant crown daisy seeds in rows. As the germination rate is bad, it is better to plant seeds in a thicker line. If you are planting in fall, plant green pak choi when crown daisy has its first thinning. If you are planting in spring, plant both crown daisy and green pak choi at the same time.

**Thinning, adding fertilizer** Crown daisy is thinned to 2–2½" (5–6 cm) between plants with 2–3 leaves, and again to 5" (12 cm) between plants when it grows 7–8 leaves. Green pak choi is thinned to two plants per spot at 1–2 leaves, and to one plant per spot at 4–5 leaves. In both cases, after second thinning, add fermented organic fertilizer.

**Harvesting** If you plant in fall, when crown daisy has about ten leaves, harvest it by pinching the tip of the stem. Leave about five lower leaves. Harvest as the side shoots grow. Thinning extends the harvest period. Green pak choi is thick and rounded and has a rounded bottom. Harvest it when the leaves grow thick.

### TIP

Because spring-planted crown daisy gets bushy easily, cut from the bottom of the plant and harvest. In the case of spring sowing, since the damage sustained by pests is small in the early stage of growth, plant crown daisy seeds and green pak choi seeds at the same time. If you start growing crown daisy earlier, you can harvest green pak choi before it starts to suffer pest damage.

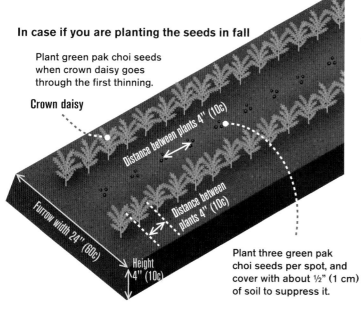

**In case if you are planting the seeds in fall**

Plant green pak choi seeds when crown daisy goes through the first thinning.

Crown daisy

Distance between plants 4" (10c)

Distance between plants 4" (10c)

Furrow width 24" (60c)

Height 4" (10c)

Plant three green pak choi seeds per spot, and cover with about ½" (1 cm) of soil to suppress it.

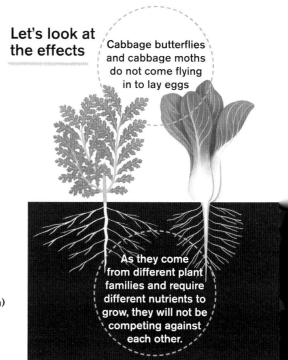

**Let's look at the effects**

Cabbage butterflies and cabbage moths do not come flying in to lay eggs

As they come from different plant families and require different nutrients to grow, they will not be competing against each other.

# Crown Daisy & Basil

## Plant basil scattered across the furrows. The scent repels pests

Pests such as plant lice or leaf miners are repelled by the unique scent of basil. Such pests are common between June to September, and basil does relatively well with heat and will protect crown daisy from pests. In addition, linalool, a chemical compound that gives basil its scent, has bactericidal effects.

It's best not to grow too many basil plants very close to the crown daisy. Especially during the summer, basil will grow tall, which prevents crown daisy from growing well. As the area of effect is wide, it is enough to plant basil every 20" (50 cm) or so.

### CULTIVATION PROCESS

**Selecting varieties** Any variety will work for crown daisy. For basil, "sweet basil" is a common and popular variety.

**Mixing soil** Three weeks before planting, add fully matured compost and fermented organic fertilizer to prepare.

**Seeding, planting** Plant crown daisy seeds in a line. In fall, you can plant seeds from early September to late October, and in spring from late March to mid-May. Planting in fall is recommended. Plant basil at the same time as the seeding of the crown daisy. When raising basil from seeds, plant seeds from the beginning of March, in a warm, sunny area. If it is to be used in the fall, you can create grafted seedlings by cutting the tip of the stems.

**Thinning, adding fertilizer** See p. 58

**Harvesting** See p. 58. Pick and harvest basil as it grows.

### TIP

When basil is picked often, the side shoots grow better, strengthening the scent and thus improving its pest repelling effect.

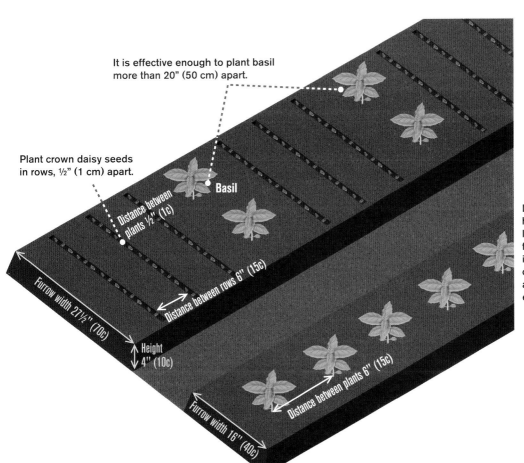

It is effective enough to plant basil more than 20" (50 cm) apart.

Plant crown daisy seeds in rows, ½" (1 cm) apart.

Basil

Distance between plants ½" (1c)

Distance between rows 6" (15c)

Furrow width 27½" (70c)

Height 4" (10c)

If you would like to harvest a lot of basil leaves, you can make a furrow for basil which is separated from the crown daisy furrow, and plant the seedlings every 10" (25 cm).

Distance between plants 6" (15c)

Furrow width 16" (40c)

# Mixed Planting of Leafy Vegetables

## Plant vegetables from different plant families to maximize the pest repelling effect

It's helpful to be able to harvest different types of leafy vegetables in small harvest sizes. Let's apply our knowledge of companion plants and cultivate multiple species at once.

Popular leafy vegetables such as Japanese mustard spinach, green pak choi, potherb mustard, and Indian mustard are all Brassicaceae family plants. If you add in small vegetables such as turnips and radishes, most of the furrow will be occupied by Brassicaceae plants. Growing these together in one spot encourages pests such as plant lice, spider mites, cabbage butterflies, cabbage moths and sawflies because all of these pests like Brassicaceae plants.

By positioning Asteraceae plants (eg. crown daisy, lettuce, chicory escarole, and Korean lettuce), Amaranthaceae plants (eg. spinach and leaf beets), Liliaceae plants or Alliaceae plants between the Brassicaceae, you place a good buffer between plants of a single family. As pests have clear preferences to the exclusion of other plants, interspersing your plant families in this way can greatly reduce pest damage.

## CULTIVATION PROCESS

**Selecting varieties** Leafy vegetables are planted late March to mid-May, or early September to mid-October. They can be harvested over a long period if you plant them at slightly different times. If you are planting in spring, choose a spring-planted variety so the cultivation does not fail.

**Mixing soil** Three weeks before planting, add fully matured compost and fermented organic fertilizer to prepare.

**Adding fertilizer** Not necessary.

**Thinning** See the columns for each plant. You can also harvest and use the cropped vegetables for other purposes.

**Harvesting** Harvest the plants as they grow large enough.

### Radish (Brassicaceae)

Radish likes soil that leans towards an acidic state. If you grow your radishes on the outer row, it is easier to check on the root size and to harvest the roots. It is recommended to harvest the radishes according to the cultivation period.
*Plant seeds every ½" (1 cm)
*Harvest them in 30–40 days.

### Green leaf lettuce (Asteraceae)

It likes soil that leans towards acidic. You can plant green leaf lettuce either from seeds or as seedlings. If you mix in red leaf lettuce, you can better repel cabbage butterflies and moths.
*If you are planting them from the seeds, plant the seeds every ½" (1 cm). Very lightly cover the seeds with soil. If you are planting seedlings, keep them about 6–8" (15–20 cm) apart.
*Harvest from the outer leaves as they grow bigger.

Distance between rows
5~6" (12~15c)

Distance between plants
6~8" (15~20c)

 Vegetables that grow well even in poor soil

## Green pak choi (Brassicaceae)

Green pak choi likes slightly acidic soil that leans towards a neutral ph, as compared to radish or green leaf lettuce.
*Plant seeds every 1" (2 cm). You can also scatter the seeds every 6" (15 cm) if you crop the plant twice.
*You can harvest the plant in 50–60 days.

## Crown daisy (Asteraceae)

Crown daisy prefers slightly acidic soil. It is recommended to plant the varieties that grows large leaves that can be harvested from the roots in spring, and to grow varieties that make a great hot pot ingredients in fall. This plant can prevent clubroot, a common problem among Brassicaceae plants.
*Plant seeds every ½" (1 cm). Crop twice to grow plants every 5" (12 cm).
*You can harvest the plants in 40–50 days. You can harvest the leaves for longer if you do some thinning.

## Japanese mustard spinach (Brassicaceae)

It likes slightly acidic to neutral soil. This plant can prevent fusarium wilt on spinach.
*Plant seeds every ½" (1 cm). Crop the plant twice to grow plants every 2–2½" (5–6 cm).
*Harvest the leaves once they grow big enough.

## Spinach (Chenopodioideae)

It likes neutral soil. As it is more likely to suffer from fusarium wilt if the soil is acidic, you can mix in limestone when you are preparing your soil.
*Plant seeds every ¼–½" (5–10 mm). Crop twice to grow the plants every 2–2½" (5–6 cm).
*Harvest the plant by the time it grows seven leaves so that flower spikes do not develop.

## Green onion (Alliaceae)

It likes slightly acidic to neutral soil. Plant seeds in plastic pots from early March to grow seedlings. It works particularly well when you plant green onion with spinach.
*Plant 2–3 seedlings about every 8–12" (20–30 cm).
*You can harvest the plant in about 30 days after planting.

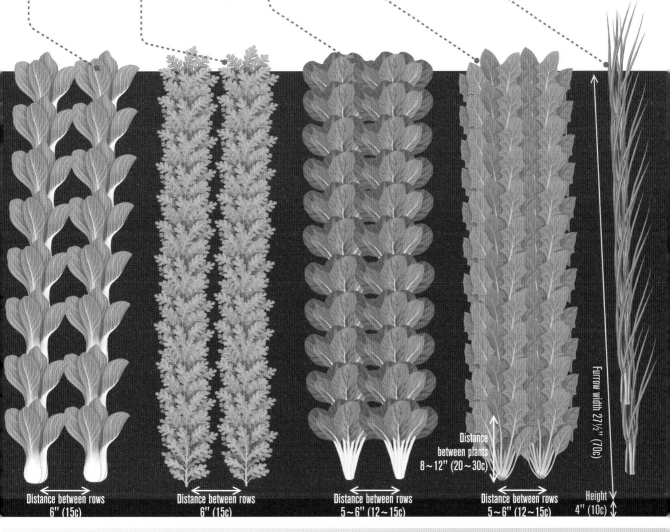

Distance between rows 6" (15c)

Distance between rows 6" (15c)

Distance between rows 5~6" (12~15c)

Distance between plants 8~12" (20~30c)

Distance between rows 5~6" (12~15c)

Furrow width 27½" (70c)

Height 4" (10c)

Vegetables that like having plenty of nutrients. As the flow of water can also bring nutrients, if your plot is on a slight slope you should keep this side lower.

# Iceberg Lettuce & Broccoli

Efficient use of space    Repels pests    Speeds up growth

## Cultivate iceberg lettuce early in spring by using broccoli as a shield from the cold

By planting iceberg lettuce behind broccoli, you can shift the cultivation period. Iceberg lettuce seedlings can handle the cold relatively well, so you can grow them from early in the spring. It is recommended to plant iceberg lettuce near broccoli so that broccoli can protect the iceberg lettuce seedlings in case of unexpected frost or cold wind. Using this method, you can start the cultivation 2–3 weeks early, and you can harvest the plants from mid-May.

Also, it is commonly known that iceberg lettuce may sustain damage from frost if you plant it early in the fall—for instance in the first half of October—but broccoli can serve as a shield from frost. Iceberg lettuce, an Asteraceae plant, and broccoli, a Brassicaceae plant are different plant types, so they can repel each other's common pests.

**Application** You can also plant cabbage or cauliflower in place of broccoli.

### CULTIVATION PROCESS

**Selecting varieties** It is safer to choose varieties of iceberg lettuce that can handle the cold. There are broccoli varieties that can allow you to start harvesting in late March to mid-April. Choose varieties according to the cultivation period.

**Mixing soil** Three weeks before planting broccoli, add fully matured compost and fermented organic fertilizer to prepare.

**Planting** Plant broccoli in October. From the beginning of March to the middle of March, plant iceberg lettuce seedlings between broccoli stocks. Grow iceberg lettuce seedlings in plastic pots in mid-February and keep it warm.

**Adding fertilizer, earthing up** When planting iceberg lettuce, add a handful of fermented organic fertilizer to the broccoli. At the same time, earth up.

**Harvesting** If you grasp the lettuce head and can feel that it has hardened, harvest it from the bottom of the plant. It is fresher when harvested early in the morning. Broccoli is harvested when the florets grow.

### TIP

If broccoli is surrounded by sufficient soil, iceberg lettuce can be planted in the gap between the broccoli rows. This environment is as effective as planting in a hole. It will be easily warmed by sunlight, and the seedlings will grow well.

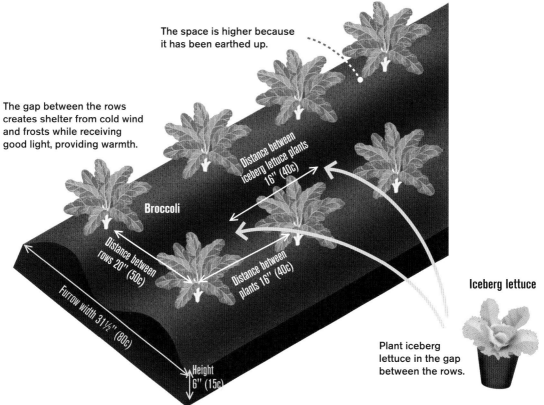

The space is higher because it has been earthed up.

The gap between the rows creates shelter from cold wind and frosts while receiving good light, providing warmth.

Distance between iceberg lettuce plants 16" (40c)

Broccoli

Distance between rows 20" (50c)

Distance between plants 16" (40c)

Furrow width 31½" (80c)

Height 6" (15c)

Iceberg lettuce

Plant iceberg lettuce in the gap between the rows.

# Garlic Chives & Fat Hen

## Use naturally grown plants to produce soft garlic chive leaves

You can grow soft garlic chive leaves if you allow fat hen, a weed that springs naturally, to grow. First, cut the garlic chive leaves that died in the winter, around mid-to-late March. Although it's still cold out, fat hen will start growing if you mow the surface of the ground around this time period.

Garlic chives' roots absorb nutrients from winter to spring, and use the stored nutrients to sustain themselves until July. During this time, fat hen will grow deep, straight roots between the garlic chives' roots, making it easier for the garlic chive roots to absorb water. In summer, fat hen will cover the ground to function as mulch and hydrate the soil. You can harvest soft and delicious garlic chive leaves from summer to fall, without the leaves hardening.

**Application** You can also use lambsquarters as an alternative.

### CULTIVATION PROCESS

**Selecting varieties** Any variety will work for garlic chives.

**Mixing soil** Three weeks before planting, add fully matured compost and fermented organic fertilizer to prepare. It is also good to add lime to the soil.

**Planting** The middle of June is the right time. Collect and plant three seedlings in one spot. Seedlings can be purchased, or you can grow them in fertile fields in late March.

**Adding fertilizer** When the leaf color of the garlic chives becomes pale, apply rice bran or a slightly immature feather fertilizer to the corner of the furrow.

**Mowing** When the plant has grown, cut the leaves back to about 1"–1½" (2–3 cm) from the base in early to mid October to keep growth soft and fragrant.

**Harvesting** Once the plant reaches 12" (30 cm), harvest it at any time, as per mowing. Harvesting is possible from mid-June to December. Frequent harvesting (4–5 times) exhausts the plant, so let it rest for two months.

**Dividing** Divide the stock every 3–4 years and replant in bunches of three.

### TIP

Fat hen leaves grow up to about 3 feet (1 m) in height when left on their own, so harvest it when leaves are close to the plant height of the garlic chives. You can also use the cut leaves as mulch.

### Let's look at the effects

Plant three garlic chives in a bunch every 4" (10 cm)

Mow down chive leaves from 1–1½" (2–3 cm) above the ground—in the same way that you do when you first cut the leaves and discard them.

**Functions as mulch**

Fat hen surrounds the space around garlic chives to function as mulch and keep soil hydrated.

Height 4" (10c)

Furrow width 16" (40c)

**Helps with extending the roots**

Fat hen grows deep roots to assist garlic chives with extending the roots.

# Onions & Fava Beans

Speeds up growth    Efficient use of space    Prevents disease    Repels pests

## Harvest these plants on the same furrow during the same cultivation period

Onions and fava beans are both planted in November and harvested in May/June. As the cultivation period is almost exactly the same, you can use the space efficiently by growing them on the same furrow.

Onions have great chemistry with Fabaceae family plants, as they support each other's roots and prevent frost from damaging the plants. Also, onions belong in the genus Allium, so the antibiotic bacteria on the roots will prevent diseases such as damping off from the fava beans.

As the temperature rises, the plants will attract lice; however, this will also attract beneficial insects such as ladybugs and marmalade hoverflies, allowing fava beans to function as a banker plant. As the days grow even warmer, the root nodule bacteria on the fava beans will also actively capture the nitrogen in the atmosphere to enrich the soil nearby. Onions will absorb these nutrients from the soil to enlarge the onion bulbs.

**Application** You can also use peas instead of fava beans, as they have a similar cultivation period.

### CULTIVATION PROCESS

**Selecting varieties** Any variety will work for both plants.

**Planting, raising seedlings** The onion is planted by raising seeds using the corner of the field. The planting season is September, but it depends on the variety, as some are early-maturing while others are late-maturing. Commercially available seedlings can also be used. For fava beans plant one seed per plastic pot from late October to early November.

**Mixing soil** Three weeks before planting, add fully matured compost and fermented organic fertilizer to prepare.

**Planting** The onion is planted when the plant height is about 6" (15 cm). Distance between stock is generally 6" (15 cm), but it may be packed to about 4" (10 cm). Plant fava bean seedlings when they have 2–3 leaves after the cotyledon.

**Adding fertilizer** For onion, add rice bran or fermented organic fertilizer once in mid to late December and once at the end of February, and mix it with the soil. Fava beans do not require added fertilizer

**Harvesting** When about 80% of the onion tops fall over, harvest them all including those that aren't yet "tops down." Harvest fava bean pods when they are full.

### TIP

This is a simple way to plant onions on both sides of fava beans. Conversely, fava beans can be placed on a wide onion furrow.

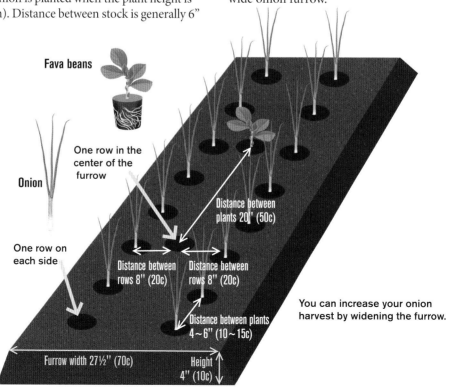

Fava beans

Onion

One row in the center of the furrow

One row on each side

Distance between plants 20" (50c)

Distance between rows 8" (20c)

Distance between rows 8" (20c)

Distance between plants 4~6" (10~15c)

Furrow width 27½" (70c)

Height 4" (10c)

You can increase your onion harvest by widening the furrow.

# Let's look at the effects

**Functions as a banker plant**

Although fava bean stems tend to have plant lice in early spring, they will also attract natural enemies such as ladybugs to kill the pests on onions.

**Functions as mulch**

Onion can grow well under the fava beans, which create a bit of shade and hydrate the soil near the base.

**Prevent diseases for fava beans**

Mycorrhizal fungi on the onion roots can prevent fusarium wilt on fava beans.

**Speed up the growth of onions**

When spring comes, fava beans spread new roots which will enrich the soil with newly acquired root nodule bacteria.

# Onions & Crimson Clover

## Mix-cultivate Fabaceae plants to grow large onions

Crimson clover is a Fabaceae green manure crop. It will grow short and sprawling, creating ground cover to prevent onions from suffering frost damage.

In March, the clover will start growing rapidly and prevent other types of weeds from growing. Soft leaves of crimson clover may have plant lice in the early days, but will soon turn into a habitat for beneficial insects like ladybugs. Root nodule bacteria on the roots will capture nitrogen in the atmosphere to enrich the soil nearby. Onions will use the nutrients from the soil to grow large bulbs.

### CULTIVATION PROCESS

**Selecting varieties** Any variety can work for onion. Crimson clover is commercially available for green manure and is also sold as a flower seed.

**Seeding, growing seedlings** Grow onion seedlings using corners of the furrow. The planting season for onion is September, though planting time varies by variety. Commercially available seedlings can also be used.

**Mixing soil** Three weeks before planting, add fully matured compost and fermented organic fertilizer to prepare.

**Planting, seeding** Onions are planted with a seedling of about 6" (15 cm) in height from mid-November to early in December. Depending on the variety, planting too early will cause bolting. After planting, sprinkle the seeds of crimson clover on the furrow and mix lightly with the soil.

**Adding fertilizer** As crimson clover enriches the soil, you do not have to add fertilizer. If the soil is poor, see p. 64 for adding a bit of fertilizer.

**Harvesting** See p. 64

### TIP

Crimson clover produces bright red flowers in late April and seeds in mid May. It can become invasive, so take care to manage it properly. It dies off in winter, but if necessary you can avoid regrowth by mowing it after the early bud stage.

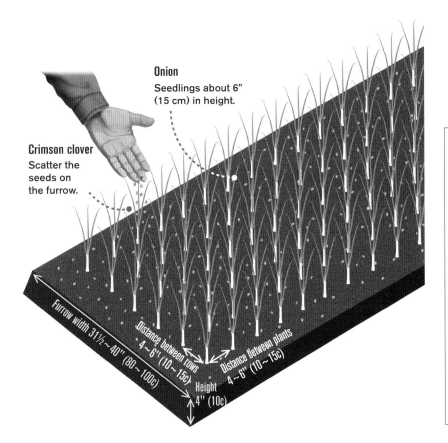

**Onion**
Seedlings about 6" (15 cm) in height.

**Crimson clover**
Scatter the seeds on the furrow.

Furrow width 31½ ~ 40" (80 ~ 100c)

Distance between rows 4 ~ 6" (10 ~ 15c)

Distance between plants 4 ~ 6" (10 ~ 15c)

Height 4" (10c)

**Also works as a banker plant**
Crimson clover starts growing flower spikes around early to mid-April. If you cut the flower spikes, the plant will stay youthful, and you can keep cultivating the plant until summer. Once the plant gets big enough, it will play the role of a banker plant to attract beneficial insects. Crimson clover is used as a banker plant for the cultivation of tomatoes in the picture.

# Onions & Chamomile

Repels pests

## Scent of the herbs repels pests on the onions

You'll notice that sometimes onion leaves become white. This is a probably a symptom thrips, a common garden vegetable pest that sucks the juices scrapes the fruits, flowers and leaves, inhibiting photosynthesis and therefore slowing the plant's growth.

Thrips hate the smell of chamomile, so pairing chamomile with onion will keep thrips at bay. Chamomile can also keep plant lice off the onions as it serves as a home to both plant lice and ladybugs.

**Application** You can expect the same effect when you plant cucumber instead of onions.

### CULTIVATION PROCESS

**Selecting varieties** Any variety will work for onion. For chamomile, small varieties are easiest.

**Seeding, raising seedlings** For onion, see p. 66. Plant chamomile seeds in the latter half of September in a nursery box. You can also use commercially sold seedlings.

**Mixing soil** Three weeks before planting onions, add fully matured compost and fermented organic fertilizer to prepare.

**Planting** For onion see p. 66. Plant one chamomile seedling for every 4–5 onion seedlings.

**Adding fertilizer** For onions, add rice bran or fermented organic fertilizer once in mid to late December and once at the end of February, mixing lightly with the soil. Do the same for chamomile.

**Watering** If you are experiencing a dry winter, watering the plant frequently aids the plant's growth.

**Harvesting** See p. 64 for onion. If you cut the tip of the grown leaves in mid to late March, the side shoots increase and many flowers result. It blooms from the beginning of April to the middle of May, so you can enjoy the smell by picking the flowers that have begun to bloom.

### TIP

The variety knowns as Roman chamomile is a perennial plant, low in height, with a strong aroma not only from the flowers but also from the stems and leaves. It may be planted collectively around a ridge or field that is upwind. As it cannot handle the heat, cut the plant back in the summer for ventilation.

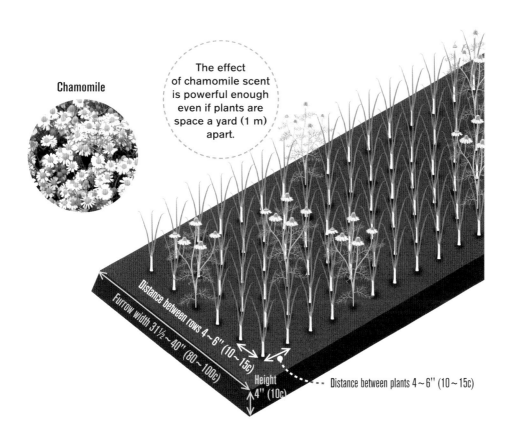

Chamomile

The effect of chamomile scent is powerful enough even if plants are space a yard (1 m) apart.

Distance between rows 4~6" (10~15c)

Furrow width 31½~40" (80~100c)

Distance between plants 4~6" (10~15c)

Height 4" (10c)

# Photo Examples of Companion Plants

Cultivation using companion plants has been practiced in many places. Here, we use photos to introduce you to some typical combinations.

**Repels pests**

### Repel pests on Brassicaceae plants

Plant red leaf lettuce, an Asteraceae plant, every 3–4 broccoli (a Brassicaceae plant). This can minimize the damage sustained by pests such as cabbage butterflies and moths.

Plant salvia, a Labiatae plant, in-between broccoli. You can take advantage not only of the scent but also of the color red, which cabbage butterflies and moths avoid.

### Intercrop vegetables from different plant families

You can prevent pest damage by planting vegetables from different plant families together. From left: Crown daisy (Asteraceae), Japanese mustard spinach (Brassicaceae), green leaf lettuce (Asteraceae), spinach (Chenopodioideae), carrot (Umbelliferae), green pak choi (Brassicaceae).

### Create a habitat for natural enemies

Intercropping of green pepper and marigold. Marigold plays the role of banker plant to increase the number of natural enemies that can kill plant lice, thrips and spider mites.

## Prevents Disease

### Plant garlic chives with Solanaceae plants

Plant garlic chives at the foot of tomato plants. Mycorrhizal fungi on Alliaceae plants decrease wilt-disease-causing bacteria.

### Plant scallions with Cucurbitae plants

Mycorrhizal fungi on Alliaceae roots can positively affect Cucurbitae plants. Above, scallions are grown at the foot of muskmelon plants.

### Prevent clubroot in Brassicaceae plants

Cultivate oats surrounding Chinese cabbage. Oats release a bactericidal substance from the roots, preventing clubroot, a common problem among Brassicaceae plants.

### Prevent powdery mildew

Grow mulch-wheat on the walkways between cucumber furrows. Plants similar to wheat can increase the number of mycoparasites that kill powdery-mildew-causing bacteria. It can also become a banker plant to house natural enemies.

## Speeds up growth

### Mix-plant or intercrop Fabaceae plants

Plant peanuts on the corner of a tomato furrow. The root nodule bacteria on Fabaceae plant roots can enrich the soil. The stems and leaves can serve as mulch.

Intercropping between corn and edamame. Fabaceae root nodule bacteria can enrich the soil, and at the same time, develops a network of nutrients between plants to induce each other's growth.

### Improve quality by mix-planting

As green onion can prevent overload of nutrients, you can harvest tasty spinach.

### Increase the size of harvest

Planting garlic with strawberry can increase the size of the harvest because garlic induces floral differentiation. Planting petunia with strawberry will attract flower-visiting insects to pollinate the flowers.

## Efficient use of space

### Actively use the empty space around the base

Grow parsley using the empty space under the eggplant plant. As parsley leaves spread over the ground, it can also keep the soil hydrated.

### Use the plant as a shield from the cold

Plant fava beans near spring-harvested cabbage. Cabbage can protect fava beans from the cold wind, and cabbage can be harvested before fava beans are harvested.

### Use the shade created by the plant

You can grow daikon in summer if you plant in the shade created by taro leaves.

### Use the plant as trellis

Grow peas by allowing the vines to grow around dead okra stems. In winter, okra can protect peas from the cold wind.

# Turnips & Green Onion

## Grow sweet turnips with delicious leaves

Brassicaceae and Alliaceae plants have different types of pests that repel each other, so planting these families together will reduce pest damage. Also, as these plants have different types of bacteria on the roots, pairing them can prevent diseases.

Green onion likes to absorb ammonia nitrogen, while turnip likes nitrate nitrogen. They will not be competing for the nutrients, and they will not suffer from an overload of fertilizer. As a result, turnips grow round and sweet, and the leaves will not have a harsh taste.

**Application** You can also grow Brassicaceae plants such as green pak choi, Japanese mustard spinach or spinach instead of turnip. You can grow chives in place of green onion.

## CULTIVATION PROCESS

**Selecting varieties** Any variety can work for both plants. You can grow any size of turnip if you adjust the distance between rows.

**Mixing soil** Three weeks before planting seeds and seedlings, add mature compost and fermented organic fertilizer into the soil and prepare a furrow.

**Seeding of turnip, Planting green onion** You can plant them at the same time. Ideal timing is late March to early April if you are planting them in spring, and the latter half of September if you are planting in fall. Distance between turnip rows is about 6" (15 cm). Plant turnip seeds in a line, ½" (1 cm) apart. Keep the distance between green onion at 6" (15 cm).

**Thinning** Thin the turnip to a distance of app. 1½" (3 cm) at one leaf, 2" (5 cm) at three leaves. Once turnip starts enlarging the roots, you can thin the plant even more to keep 4" (10 cm) between each plant. You can also eat the thinned plant.

**Adding fertilizer** Not necessary.

**Harvesting** Harvest turnip once it grows to about 2–3" (5–8 cm) in diameter. Green onion leaves are harvested leaving 1½–2" (3–5 cm) from the stock origin. The leaves will regrow.

### TIP

If green onions are grown from young seedlings, they will grow well if planted in triplicate. When transplanting a thick one, plant one per spot. After the turnips are harvested, they may be dug up and moved to another place for later.

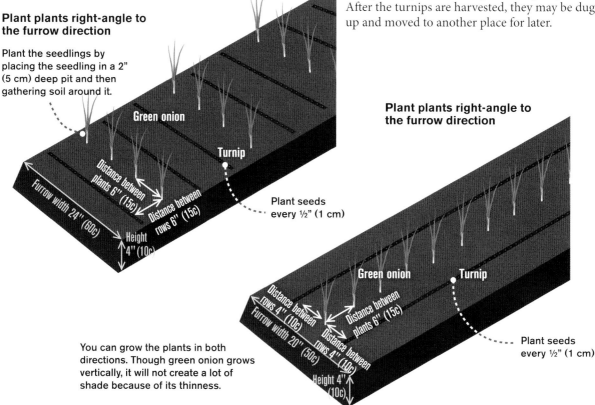

**Plant plants right-angle to the furrow direction**

Plant the seedlings by placing the seedling in a 2" (5 cm) deep pit and then gathering soil around it.

Green onion

Turnip

Distance between plants 6" (15c)

Distance between rows 6" (15c)

Furrow width 24" (60c)

Height 4" (10c)

Plant seeds every ½" (1 cm)

You can grow the plants in both directions. Though green onion grows vertically, it will not create a lot of shade because of its thinness.

**Plant plants right-angle to the furrow direction**

Green onion

Turnip

Distance between rows 4" (10c)

Distance between plants 6" (15c)

Distance between rows 4" (10c)

Furrow width 20" (50c)

Height 4" (10c)

Plant seeds every ½" (1 cm)

# Turnips & Green Leaf Lettuce

Repels pests

## Prevent cabbage butterflies and cabbage moths from landing on turnips using the scent of an Asteraceae plant

This is a pairing of turnip, a Brassicaceae plant, with green leaf lettuce, an Asteraceae plant. As they are from different plant families, they will repel each other's pests. Although turnips tend to suffer severe damage caused by cabbage butterflies or cabbage moths, green leaf lettuce can repel these pests. In addition, the plant lice that are attracted to green leaf lettuce are repelled by the scent of turnips, so they will avoid both plants.

It is effective enough to plant one row of green leaf lettuce for every 4–5 rows of turnip. As green leaf lettuce spreads onto the sides, it is recommended to keep a little more distance between lettuce seedlings than between turnip seedlings.

**Application** You can also plant crown daisy instead of green leaf lettuce. It is also effective to plant green pak choi, Japanese mustard spinach or potherb spinach in lieu of turnip.

### CULTIVATION PROCESS

**Selecting varieties** Turnip and leaf lettuce can be any variety. Red leaf lettuce is a good option, as pests dislike the color.

**Mixing soil** Three weeks before planting seeds and seedlings, add mature compost and fermented organic fertilizer into the soil and prepare a furrow.

**Seeding of turnip, planting of green leaf lettuce** You can plant them at the same time. Ideal timing is late March to early April you are planting them in spring, and the latter half of September if you are planting in fall. Keep the distance between rows at 8" (20 cm). You can plant turnip seeds in a line, one seed every ½" (1 cm). Keep the distance between green leaf lettuce at 6" (15 cm).

**Thinning** See p. 70.

**Adding fertilizer** Not necessary.

**Harvesting** See p. 70. You can harvest green leaf lettuce for a longer period of time if you only harvest the outer leaves. You can harvest the whole plant as well.

### TIP

Particularly effective in fall. The turnips may not be harvested if they are damaged by pests before they reach maturity, so it is better to plant leaf lettuce from seedlings beforehand.

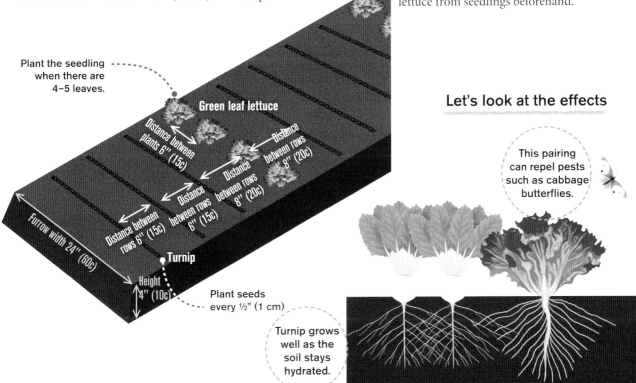

Plant the seedling when there are 4–5 leaves.

Green leaf lettuce

Distance between plants 6" (15c)

Distance between rows 8" (20c)

Distance between rows 8" (20c)

Distance between rows 6" (15c)

Distance between rows 6" (15c)

Furrow width 24" (60c)

Turnip

Height 4" (10c)

Plant seeds every ½" (1 cm)

Turnip grows well as the soil stays hydrated.

### Let's look at the effects

This pairing can repel pests such as cabbage butterflies.

# Daikon & Marigold

Repels pests    Speeds up growth

## Reduce meadow nematode around the roots by preventing pests above the ground

The unique scent of marigold can repel pests such as cabbage butterflies and cabbage moths on Brassicaceae plants.

Because pest damage becomes severe as it gets warmer, it is the most effective to plant marigold with daikon that is planted in mid-June, which at one time was considered hard to do. Marigold can reduce pest damage to daikon even when it is planted in September, as it can protect daikon during the first stage of growth.

Also, meadow nematode creates black spots and lowers the daikon's quality; however, meadow nematode is even more attracted to marigold; therefore, the daikon is protected.

**Application** You can also plant Solanaceae plants such as eggplants or green pepper, or Brassicaceae plants such as cabbage, broccoli and Chinese cabbage to benefit from the pest repellent effect of marigold. You can also use carrot or greater burdock as a solution to meadow nematode.

### CULTIVATION PROCESS

**Selecting varieties** Any variety works for daikon. African varieties of marigold are a better companion choice than French ones.

**Mixing soil** Make a furrow three weeks before planting daikon. Do not add any fertilizer.

**Seeding, planting** The radish is planted with 5–7 grains in one place. If you want to raise marigold from seed, plant after the beginning of April. Seedlings are planted when there are 4–5 leaves after the cotyledon.

**Thinning** Daikon is thinned to three plants per spot when there is one leaf after cotyledon, then again to two plants per spot when there are 3–4 leaves, then down to one plant per spot after 6–7 leaves.

**Adding fertilizer** Not necessary.

**Earthing up** If you are growing a daikon variety whose roots poke out of the soil, earth up.

**Harvesting** Harvest daikon according to the harvest date determined by the variety. Usually about 60–70 days. It takes longer if you plant in fall.

### TIP

If the damage from meadow nematode is severe, you can plant marigold from spring to summer, then plant daikon three weeks after raking the marigold leaves into the soil as green manure. If you do this once every few years, it is possible to harvest daikon all year.

# Daikon & Arugula

Efficient use of space    Repels pests    Speeds up growth

## Grow one more plant that has short cultivation period

Using the space between rows of daikon, this method allows you to harvest one more type of plant. Daikon has a cultivation period of about 60–70 days. If you plant them in late September, the cultivation period is longer. Arugula seeds can be planted in the latter half of fall; this plant has a cultivation period of just 30–40 days. By the time arugula has grown mature and is harvested, daikon will need the extra space it vacates to grow leaves and enlarge the root.

**Application** You can maximize space and time by adding small turnips, which have short cultivation period. Harvesting serves to thin the plants.

### CULTIVATION PROCESS

**Selecting varieties** Can be any variety.

**Mixing soil** Prepare a furrow three weeks before planting. Do not add any fertilizer.

**Seeding** Plant 5–7 daikon seeds per spot. You can either plant arugula seeds in a line, or scattered across the plot.

**Thinning** Thinning method for daikon is as explained-above. Frequently thin the plant and use them in salads.

**Adding fertilizer** Not necessary.

**Harvesting** For daikon, see above. Harvest when roots grow large. Harvest all arugula after 40 days.

### TIP

The chickweed that grows in the fall is compatible with Brassicaceae vegetables, and if left in place, it will cover the surface as mulch, helping soil stay hydrated. Arugula is an alternative to chickweed.

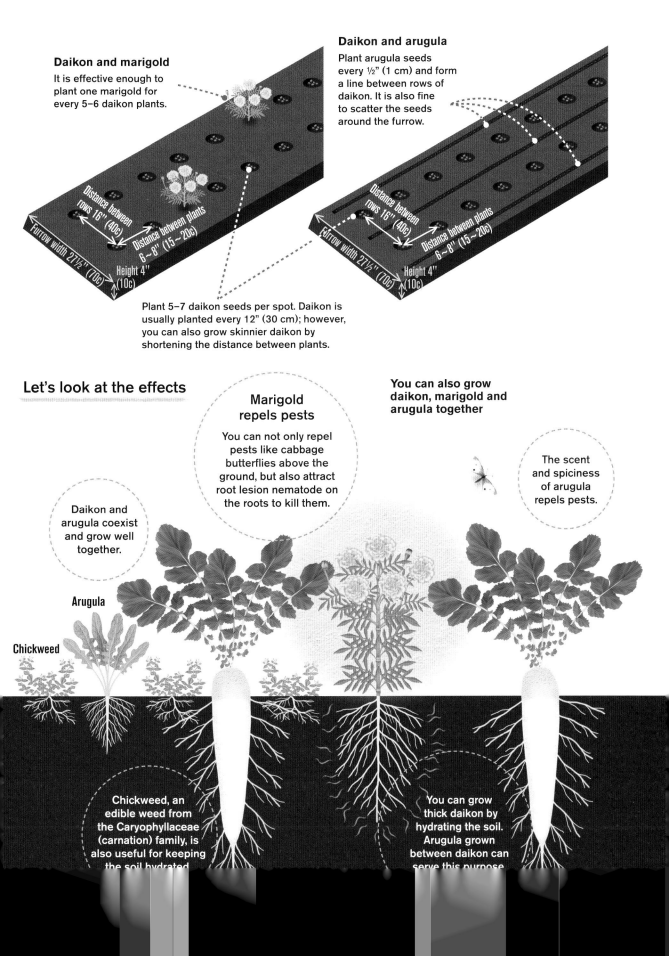

## Daikon and marigold

It is effective enough to plant one marigold for every 5–6 daikon plants.

## Daikon and arugula

Plant arugula seeds every ½" (1 cm) and form a line between rows of daikon. It is also fine to scatter the seeds around the furrow.

Distance between rows 16" (40c)

Distance between plants 6~8" (15~20c)

Furrow width 27½" (70c)

Height 4" (10c)

Distance between rows 16" (40c)

Distance between plants 6~8" (15~20c)

Furrow width 27½" (70c)

Height 4" (10c)

Plant 5–7 daikon seeds per spot. Daikon is usually planted every 12" (30 cm); however, you can also grow skinnier daikon by shortening the distance between plants.

## Let's look at the effects

### Marigold repels pests

You can not only repel pests like cabbage butterflies above the ground, but also attract root lesion nematode on the roots to kill them.

### You can also grow daikon, marigold and arugula together

The scent and spiciness of arugula repels pests.

Daikon and arugula coexist and grow well together.

Arugula

Chickweed

Chickweed, an edible weed from the Caryophyllaceae (carnation) family, is also useful for keeping the soil hydrated.

You can grow thick daikon by hydrating the soil. Arugula grown between daikon can serve this purpose.

# Radish & Basil

## Protect radishes with short cultivation periods from pests by using the scent of basil

Radish has a short cultivation period of 40 days, so while it requires little effort, it often attracts unexpected numbers of pests. Although radish leaves don't serve any particular purpose, if they are consumed by pests, the plant's roots cannot recover from the damage during the short cultivation period and, as a result, the root hardens without getting bigger.

If you plant a Labiatae plant such as basil at the same time as radishes, the unique scent can protect the radish all the way from the first stage of growth to harvest period. It is effective enough to plant one basil seedling every 20" (50 cm).

**Application** You can plant basil with other Brassicaceae plants, Asteraceae plants such as lettuce and crown daisy, or Solanaceae plants such as eggplants and tomatoes.

### CULTIVATION PROCESS

**Selecting varieties** Any variety can work for both plants.

**Mixing soil** Not necessary if the soil is rich. If the soil is poor, add mature compost and fermented organic fertilizer, mixing it into the soil three weeks before planting, and prepare a furrow.

**Seeding, Planting** Plant radish in mid-March to late May if planted in spring, or late August to late October if planted in fall. Either plant the seeds in a row or plant three seeds per spot. Plant basil when it has 4–6 leaves. If you are growing a seedling, plant seeds in a plastic pot at the beginning of March, and lightly cover the seeds with soil. You can also use commercially bought seedlings.

**Thinning** Thin the radish plants to a distance of 1–1½" (2–3 cm) when plants have one leaf, and 2–2½" (5–6 cm) when they have three leaves.

**Nipping** Cut the basil stem from two top nodes once the basil has 8–10 leaves. When flower buds appear, pinch them off in order to keep the leaves soft.

**Adding fertilizer** Not necessary.

**Harvesting** Harvest radish in about 40 days once the roots are big enough. Roots may split or harden if you harvest them too late.

### TIP

You can replant basil elsewhere after harvesting radishes. You can multiply basil seedlings if you plant the nipped stems.

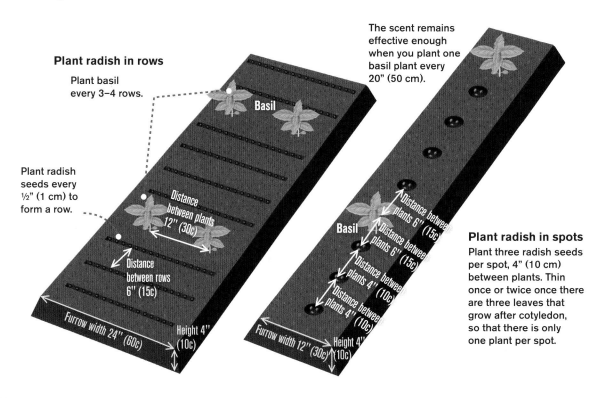

**Plant radish in rows**

Plant basil every 3–4 rows.

Plant radish seeds every ½" (1 cm) to form a row.

Basil

Distance between plants 12" (30c)

Distance between rows 6" (15c)

Furrow width 24" (60c)

Height 4" (10c)

The scent remains effective enough when you plant one basil plant every 20" (50 cm).

Basil

Distance between plants 6" (15c)
Distance between plants 6" (15c)
Distance between plants 4" (10c)
Distance between plants 4" (10c)

Furrow width 12" (30c)

Height 4" (10c)

**Plant radish in spots**
Plant three radish seeds per spot, 4" (10 cm) between plants. Thin once or twice once there are three leaves that grow after cotyledon, so that there is only one plant per spot.

# Carrots & Edamame

## A great combo for vegetables planted in summer and harvested in fall. Grows well without much fertilizer

Plant seeds of both carrots and edamame in early stages of summer. The unique scent of an Umbelliferae plant like carrot will repel stink bugs that are attracted to edamame. At the same time, you can reduce the damage from swallowtail butterflies on the carrots.

The quality of carrots drops when a lot of raw organic matter is in the soil. Rather, carrots grow big and tasty when little fertilizer is added to the soil. Start the edamame first, because it grows well even in poor soil environment. As the root nodule bacteria enriches the soil nearby, it becomes easier for carrots to absorb the nutrients and grow. Edamame roots also have mycorrhizal fungus, so they will create a network of nutrients with carrot roots as well. By the time edamame has flowers, carrots will have grown leaves that cover up the ground to keep the soil moist. This helps ensure that edamame produces great flowers and, later, great soybeans.

### CULTIVATION PROCESS

**Selecting varieties** Any variety will work for carrots. Edamame is easiest if you use early to middle varieties. If you want to plant a late carrot variety, make the edamame a late variety as well.

**Mixing soil** Prepare a furrow three weeks before planting edamame. Do not add any fertilizer.

**Seeding** Sow three edamame per spot. If growing seedlings, plant three seeds per pot and thin to two plants. Plant seedlings when there are 1½ leaves after the cotyledon. Sow carrots at the same time or slightly after thinning. Carrots are planted from late June to mid July to aim for harvesting in the fall of October to November.

**Thinning of carrots** See p. 76.

**Adding fertilizer** Not necessary.

**Earthing up** If the soil of the walkway is gathered several times at the foot of the edamame plants, the growth can be improved.

**Harvesting** Harvest edamame as it grows the beans inside the pots. Harvest according to the variety. The ideal time for harvesting carrots is 100–120 days after planting. Harvest once the roots fatten.

### TIP

Carrots can be stably grown if you use the edamame leaves and stems as mulch.

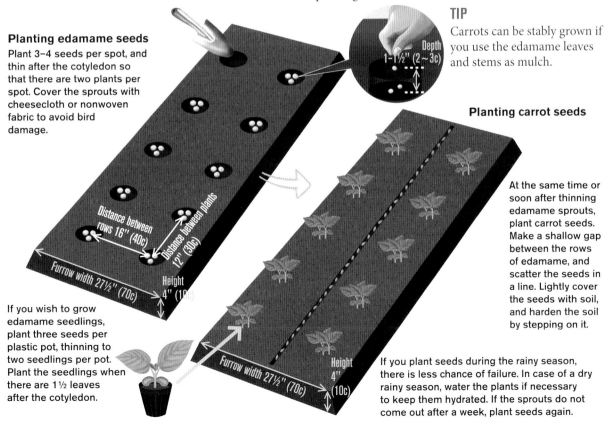

**Planting edamame seeds**
Plant 3–4 seeds per spot, and thin after the cotyledon so that there are two plants per spot. Cover the sprouts with cheesecloth or nonwoven fabric to avoid bird damage.

Depth 1–1½" (2~3c)

**Planting carrot seeds**

Distance between rows 16" (40c)

Distance between plants 12" (30c)

Furrow width 27½" (70c)

Height 4" (10c)

If you wish to grow edamame seedlings, plant three seeds per plastic pot, thinning to two seedlings per pot. Plant the seedlings when there are 1½ leaves after the cotyledon.

Furrow width 27½" (70c)

Height 4" (10c)

At the same time or soon after thinning edamame sprouts, plant carrot seeds. Make a shallow gap between the rows of edamame, and scatter the seeds in a line. Lightly cover the seeds with soil, and harden the soil by stepping on it.

If you plant seeds during the rainy season, there is less chance of failure. In case of a dry rainy season, water the plants if necessary to keep them hydrated. If the sprouts do not come out after a week, plant seeds again.

# Carrots & Daikon, Radish

Repels pests    Speeds up growth

## Grow two root vegetables by combining plants from different plant families

Carrots and daikon both have straight roots that do not interfere each other. They also grow well in soil with little fertilizer. Though they are both root vegetables, carrot is a Umbelliferae plant and daikon is a Brassicaceae plant. As they come from different plant families, they attract pests that are mutually repellant. As a result, you can prevent the damage sustained by swallowtail butterflies on carrots while preventing damage to daikon by cabbage butterflies and cabbage moths.

The cultivation period of carrot is about 100–120 days, and for daikon it is about 60–70 days. You can plant them simultaneously if you plant the seeds in late March to mid-April, for spring cultivation. If you wish to grow your plants in fall, plant carrots in mid-July to mid-August and daikon in September.
**Application** You can plant radish instead of daikon. Their short cultivation period takes place during the carrots' first stage of growth. After they are harvested, carrots make use of the vacated space.

### CULTIVATION PROCESS

**Selecting varieties** If planting in spring, choose one that doesn't easily become bushy. If planting in summer to fall, any variety will work for both plants.

**Mixing soil** Prepare a furrow three weeks before planting edamame. Do not add any fertilizer.

**Seeding** Plant carrots in a line. Plant 5–7 daikon seeds per spot.

**Thinning** Thin the carrots to space plants at 2–2½" (5–6 cm) when the plant is 1½– 2" (4–5 cm) tall, and again for a distance of 4–5" (10–12 cm) when the roots are ¼" (5 mm) thick. Thin the radish plants so that the there are three plants per spot when plants have one leaf, two plants per spot at 3–4 leaves and one per spot at 6–7 leaves.

**Adding fertilizer** Not necessary.

**Earthing up** For daikon varieties with protruding roots, earth up.

**Harvesting** Ideal harvesting for carrots is 100–120 days after planting seeds. Harvest daikon according to the variety.

### TIP

Sowing in September will reduce pest damage. In this case, plant carrots and radish simultaneously. Harvest radish from early to mid December, and carrot from late December to February in the following year.

# Carrots & Turnip, Green Pak Choi

Repels pests    Speeds up growth

## Repel pests by growing the plants closely and letting the leaves touch

This another pairing of an Umbelliferae and a Brassicaceae. For good pest control, keep the distance between plants smaller than as per daikon outlined above, allowing the plants' leaves to touch.

Both turnips and green pak choi can be harvested around 50–60 days after planting seeds. Plant them at different times so that the cultivation period overlaps properly with the carrots. If you are growing plants in spring, you can plant turnips or green pak choi from late March to early June. Between summer and fall, you can grow carrots first and then plant turnips or green pak choi in September or October.
**Application** You can also pair carrots with Japanese mustard spinach.

### CULTIVATION PROCESS

**Selecting varieties** If planting in spring, choose a variety that will not grow bushy. Any variety works if you are planting in fall.

**Mixing soil** Prepare a furrow three weeks before planting. Do not add any fertilizer.

**Seeding** Plant seeds directly in the soil, forming a line. You can also plant green pak choi in spots.

**Thinning** See above for the thinning of carrots. Thin the turnip plants to a distance of app. 1½" (3 cm) when plants have one leaf, 2" (5 cm) when there are three leaves. Once turnip roots start to grow large, thin again to a distance of 4" (10 cm).

**Adding fertilizer** Not really necessary, but if the turnip or green pak choi leaves are yellowing, add a little bit of fermented organic fertilizer.

**Harvesting** See above for carrots. Harvest turnip when it grows to about 2–3" (5–8 cm) and harvest green pak choi when bottom leaves have thickened.

### TIP

The effect of pest control can be obtained even if carrots, turnips, and pak choi are alternately grown in rows.

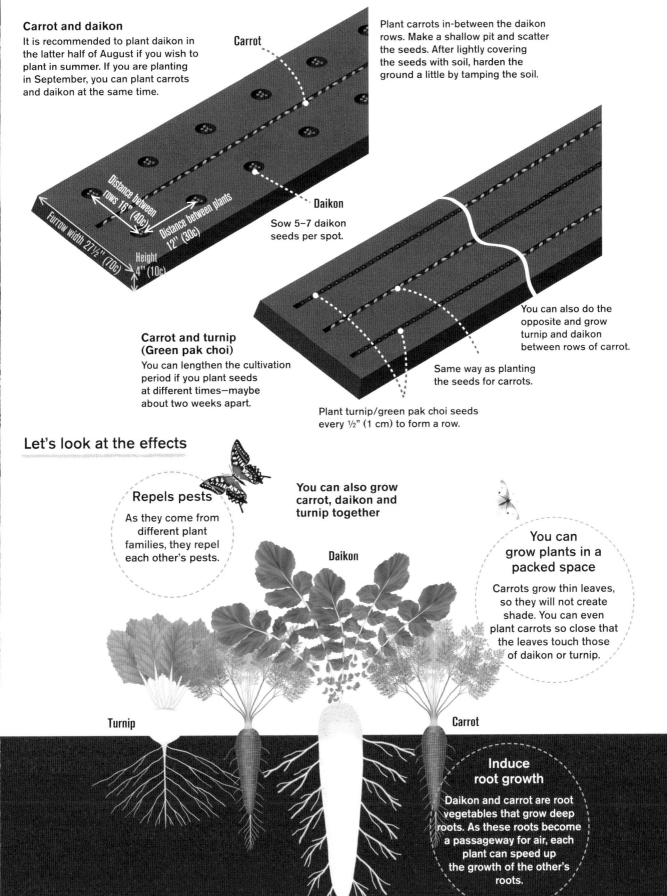

### Carrot and daikon

It is recommended to plant daikon in the latter half of August if you wish to plant in summer. If you are planting in September, you can plant carrots and daikon at the same time.

Plant carrots in-between the daikon rows. Make a shallow pit and scatter the seeds. After lightly covering the seeds with soil, harden the ground a little by tamping the soil.

Carrot

Distance between rows 16" (40c)

Distance between plants 12" (30c)

Furrow width 27½" (70c)

Height 4" (10c)

Daikon

Sow 5–7 daikon seeds per spot.

### Carrot and turnip (Green pak choi)

You can lengthen the cultivation period if you plant seeds at different times—maybe about two weeks apart.

You can also do the opposite and grow turnip and daikon between rows of carrot.

Same way as planting the seeds for carrots.

Plant turnip/green pak choi seeds every ½" (1 cm) to form a row.

## Let's look at the effects

### Repels pests

As they come from different plant families, they repel each other's pests.

### You can also grow carrot, daikon and turnip together

Daikon

### You can grow plants in a packed space

Carrots grow thin leaves, so they will not create shade. You can even plant carrots so close that the leaves touch those of daikon or turnip.

Turnip

Carrot

### Induce root growth

Daikon and carrot are root vegetables that grow deep roots. As these roots become a passageway for air, each plant can speed up the growth of the other's roots.

# Sweet Potatoes & Red Perilla

## Increase the size of your harvest by preventing vines from overgrowing—just let red perilla absorb the excess nutrients

This method is suited to gardens with rich soil. Sweet potato has mycorrhizal fungus called azospirillum that capture nitrogen in the atmosphere, so they grow well even in soil that's not nutrient-rich. Rather, when they are grown in a rich soil environment, they will only grow vines and the sweet potatoes underground will not grow large; if they do, they are often watery.

Red perilla takes enough nutrients from the sweet potatoes, preventing vine overgrowth. As the nutrients stored in the vines and leaves come back to feed the sweet potato roots, the potatoes will grow well. This method is also useful for repelling pests. Red scarab beetle worms occasionally damage the potatoes underground, but as they avoid the red color of the perilla leaves, damage is minimized.

### CULTIVATION PROCESS

**Selecting varieties** Any variety will work for sweet potatoes. You cannot expect a pest repellent effect if the perilla is not red.

**Mixing soil** Prepare a furrow two weeks before planting. A tall furrow is recommended.

**Planting** From the end of April to the end of May, seedlings (called slips) are planted vertically into the soil, leaves above ground. When vertically inserted, the slip grows round, large potatoes. When it is planted sideways, it will grow a lot of elongated potatoes. Red perilla is planted between sweet potato plants. Although seelings can be purchased, it is preferable to sow seeds in a plastic pot about 30 days before planting.

**Adding fertilizer** Not necessary.

**Removing vines** Vines sometimes grow roots when attached to the soil. Remove vines frequently to avoid wasting nutrients.

**Harvesting** Harvest after 110 days. Two to three weeks before harvest, remove the vines for the last time. Cut the vines one week before harvest to divert nutrients to the potatoes. Left on the vine, potatoes will grow larger, but their color, shape and taste will deteriorate. Red perilla can be harvested at any time by picking the tip of the stem. You can grow the perilla to be bushy if you keep picking the side shoots.

### TIP

If your field is fertile, try growing vegetables that absorb lot of fertilizer, such as spinach, before using the field for sweet potatoes. Do not fertilize the spinich.

Plant red perilla in spaces between sweet potato plants. If you also want to grow vineless black-eyed peas as shown on p. 79, plant them at the same time if the soil is malnourished. Plant three seeds per spot, and thin the sprouts so you grow one plant per spot.

It is also a good idea to grow the vines using spaces like walkways.

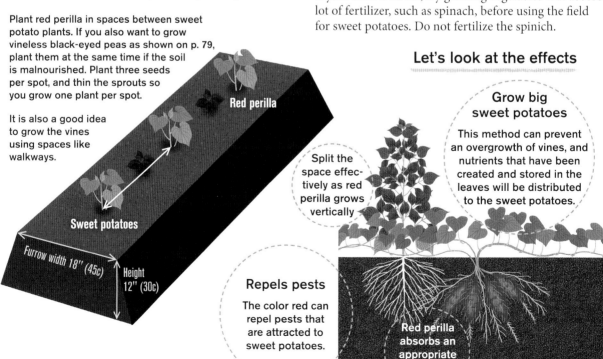

Red perilla

Sweet potatoes

Furrow width 18" (45c)

Height 12" (30c)

## Let's look at the effects

**Grow big sweet potatoes**

This method can prevent an overgrowth of vines, and nutrients that have been created and stored in the leaves will be distributed to the sweet potatoes.

**Split the space effectively as red perilla grows vertically**

**Repels pests**

The color red can repel pests that are attracted to sweet potatoes.

**Red perilla absorbs an appropriate amount of nutrients.**

# Sweet Potatoes & Vineless Black-Eyed Peas

 Efficient use of space  Speeds up growth  Repels pests

## Poor soil environment? Add a Fabaceae plant!

Sweet potatoes grow sweet and delicious when the soil is a little undernourished. In places that are sandy or otherwise low in nutrients, sweet potatoes do not suffer skin damage and the fruits are high quality.

Using the wide space dominated by the sweet potato roots, you can grow vineless black-eyed peas. Black-eyed peas are a Fabaceae plant and have root nodule bacteria on the roots, which can capture nitrogen in the air to nourish themselves. Therefore, they grow well even in poor soil conditions.

**Application** You can also use vineless green beans or edamame for mixed cultivation.

## CULTIVATION PROCESS

**Selecting varieties** Any variety can work for sweet potato. Use the vineless type of black-eyed peas.

**Mixing soil** Prepare a furrow two weeks before planting seedlings. Taller furrow is recommended.

**Slips, planting** See p. 78 for sweet potato. Plant black-eyed peas between sweet potato plants. Plant three seeds per spot.

**Thinning** Thin black-eyed peas once plants have 1–2 leaves after the cotyledon to have one plant per spot.

**Adding fertilizer** Not necessary.

**Harvesting** See p. 78 for sweet potatoes. Black-eyed peas have a long flowering period, so they will develop peapods continually. Once the pods start to become dry, harvest them. Be careful—if you leave the pods on the plant for too long, the beans will drop onto the ground.

## TIP

To avoid vine overgrowth in sweet potatoes, cultivate black-eyed peas away from the bottom of the plant, for example, in a passage that has been opened up to allow vines to extend.

## Let's look at the effects

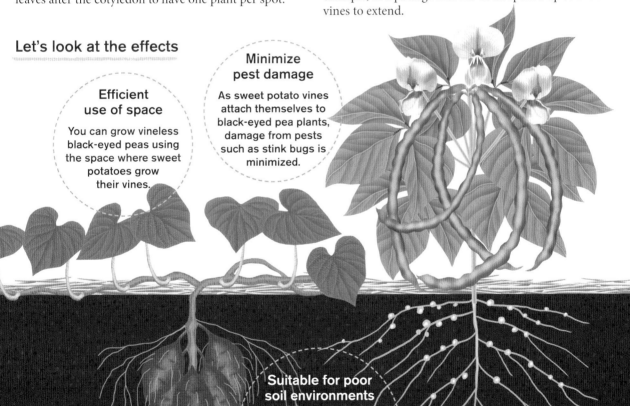

**Efficient use of space**

You can grow vineless black-eyed peas using the space where sweet potatoes grow their vines.

**Minimize pest damage**

As sweet potato vines attach themselves to black-eyed pea plants, damage from pests such as stink bugs is minimized.

**Suitable for poor soil environments**

Sweet potatoes have mycorrhizal fungi on their roots, and black-eyed peas have root nodule bacteria. Both enrich the soil, so the plants grow well even in poor soil.

# Potatoes & Taro

Efficient use of space   Speeds up growth

## Start growing taro on the furrow or on the walkways after finishing the earthing-up for the potatoes

As there are few vegetable species that can be cultivated immediately after a potato harvest, it is common to not use the space until you start growing plants again in fall. Planting with taro lets you keep the space active while you are still growing potatoes.

Taro can be grown between the rows of potatoes or on the walkways. As the position is kept low, planting taro there will not only keep the soil moist but also start growing sprouts very quickly, as the temperature is already appropriate for growing taro.

### CULTIVATION PROCESS

**Selecting varieties** Any variety can work for both plants.

**Mixing soil** Till the soil three weeks before planting taro. If the soil is not poor, fertilizer isn't necessary.

**Planting potatoes** Cut the center of the potato off, and cut the potato sideways to create about 1.5–2 oz (40–60 g) seed potatoes. Plant the seed potatoes a few days after, when the surface of the potato is completely dry.

**Thinning** If there are too many sprouts, potatoes that grow will stay small. Thin out the weak sprouts to leave 2–3 plants per spot.

**Earthing up potatoes** When the plant height is about 8" (20 cm), earth up for the first time, and again after another two weeks (generally, in the latter half of May).

**Planting taro** Taro is planted in the middle of a walkway or a row of potatoes, and covered with about 2–3" (5–7 cm) of soil. Do this after you've earthed up your potatoes for the second time.

**Harvesting potatoes** When stems and leaves are dead, dig up the potatoes to harvest.

**Earthing up taro, adding fertilizer** Gather the soil around the foot of the taro plant after digging up the potatoes. Add fermented organic fertilizer or rice bran to the surface and mix lightly. So that the soil does not dry out at the end of the rainy season, cover the ridge with straw mulch as soon as possible.

**Harvesting of taro** First half of November. Harvest before it is hit with frost.

### TIP

Since taro can be harvested sufficiently even in late June, it is possible to grow early varieties of potato and plant taro immediately after harvesting.

**1 Planting potatoes**

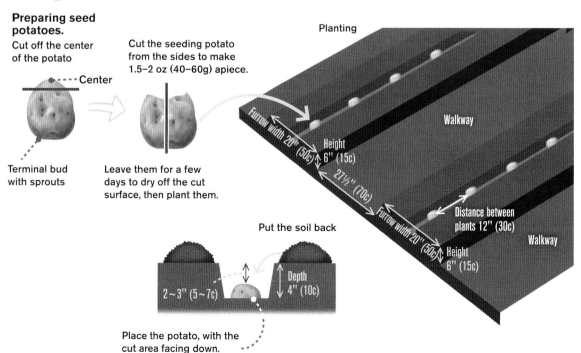

**Preparing seed potatoes.**

Cut the center off the potato

- - - - Center

Terminal bud with sprouts

Cut the seeding potato from the sides to make 1.5–2 oz (40–60g) apiece.

Leave them for a few days to dry off the cut surface, then plant them.

Put the soil back

2~3" (5~7c)   Depth 4" (10c)

Place the potato, with the cut area facing down.

Planting

Furrow width 20" (50c)

Height 6" (15c)

27½" (70c)

Walkway

Furrow width 20" (50c)

Distance between plants 12" (30c)

Height 6" (15c)

Walkway

## 2 Earthing up potatoes and planting taro

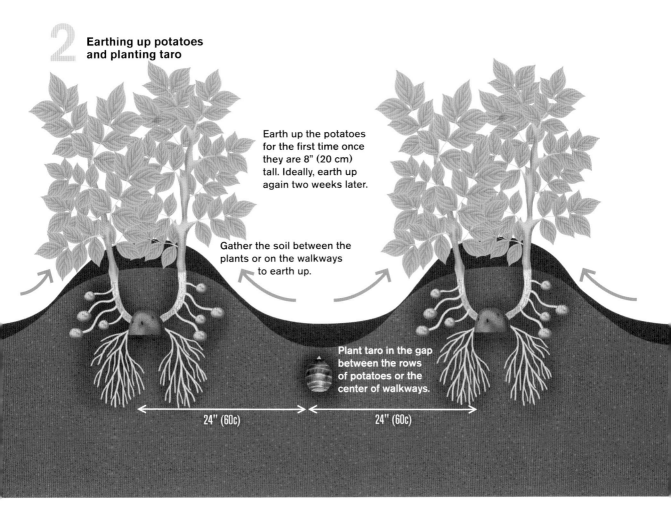

Earth up the potatoes for the first time once they are 8" (20 cm) tall. Ideally, earth up again two weeks later.

Gather the soil between the plants or on the walkways to earth up.

Plant taro in the gap between the rows of potatoes or the center of walkways.

24" (60c)

24" (60c)

## 3 Harvesting potatoes and earthing up taro

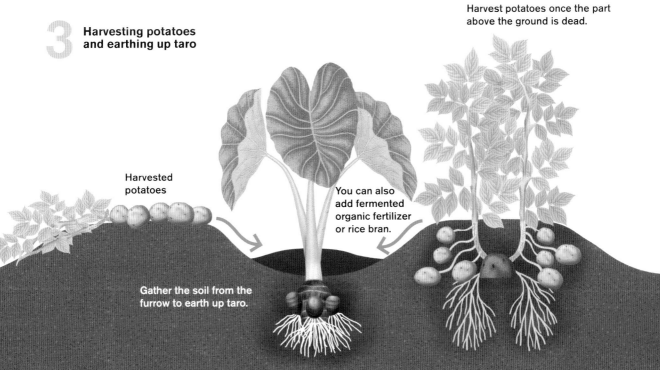

Harvest potatoes once the part above the ground is dead.

Harvested potatoes

You can also add fermented organic fertilizer or rice bran.

Gather the soil from the furrow to earth up taro.

# Potatoes & Fat Hen, Amaranth

Prevents disease

Speeds up growth

Repels pests

## Use naturally grown weed to grow disease-immune seedlings

When you till the soil to prepare a furrow for potatoes in late February to early March, weeds such as fat hen and amaranth start growing there. Both are straight-rooted plants that grow deep roots and will cover the ground with leaves to retain the soil's moisture. This will speed up the potatoes' growth. It also works to prevent dirt splatter and therefore also the blight that spatter causes.

These weeds can also protect the potato from viruses. Viruses are introduced by plant lice on the potatoes; however, only the affected area of fat hen or amaranth will die, and the virus will not spread among the weeds. Once plant lice have affected enough plants, they lose the ability to infect any others. Therefore, when lice visit weeds before moving onto the potatoes, the potatoes will not be infected.

### CULTIVATION PROCESS

**Selecting varieties** Any varieties can work.

**Mixing soil** Till the soil three weeks before planting potatoes. As long as the soil is not poor, you do not have to add any fertilizer.

**Planting** Cut the center part of the potato and cut it into 1.5–2 oz (40–60g) of seed potatoes. After a few days, dry the surface of the cuts and plant the seed potatoes. If you plant them upside down, potatoes grow well and the size of harvest will increase.

**Thinning** See p. 80. As only selected few of strong sprouts come out if the seed potato is planted upside down, you do not have to thin the sprouts.

**Earthing up potatoes** When the plant height is about 8" (20 cm), earth up for the first time, then again after another two weeks.

**Adding fertilizer** Not necessary.

**Harvesting** Once the part above the ground dies, dig up the potatoes.

### TIP

Besides attracting ladybugs, a natural enemy of plant lice, fat hen and amaranth help keep soil temperature and moisture constant, which helps potatoes to grow well. These weeds are also nutrient-rich, so when they grow tall, cutting and laying will replace green manure.

### Planting potato upside down

Sprout comes out from the bottom and grows upwards. As it receives an appropriate level of stress, it becomes more immune to diseases or climate change.

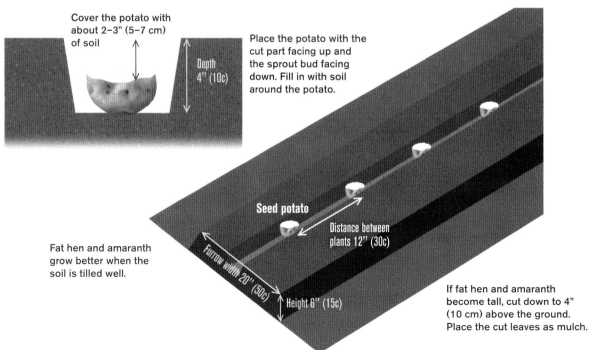

Cover the potato with about 2–3" (5–7 cm) of soil

Depth 4" (10c)

Place the potato with the cut part facing up and the sprout bud facing down. Fill in with soil around the potato.

Seed potato

Distance between plants 12" (30c)

Fat hen and amaranth grow better when the soil is tilled well.

Furrow width 20" (50c)

Height 6" (15c)

If fat hen and amaranth become tall, cut down to 4" (10 cm) above the ground. Place the cut leaves as mulch.

# Red Potatoes & Celery

## Grow tasty celery using the shade between the rows of potatoes

Similar to pairing potatoes with taro (see p. 80), this method places a different type of plant between rows of potatoes. This pairing uses red potatoes instead of spring-planted potatoes.

Fall-planted red potatoes are usually planted in early September and can be harvested during late November to mid-December, after the leaves above the ground have completely died. Celery is planted in July to September, and harvested in early November to mid-December, so you can match the cultivation periods of these plants together.

It is recommended to plant celery in an environment where there's enough shade to slightly suppress growth. You can harvest delicious stalks if you limit the light source in the latter half of cultivation. If you grow celery between rows of red potatoes, it'll have enough water to grow strong and tasty.

## CULTIVATION PROCESS

**Selecting varieties** For potatoes, select varieties suitable for fall planting such as "Dejima" and "Andean Red." Any variety will work for celery.

**Mixing soil** Prepare a furrow three weeks before planting. No need to add any fertilizer. Till the soil where celery will be planted.

**Planting** Potato seeds are 1.5–2 (40–60g) each. In the case of fall potatoes, cutting the potato invites rot, so plant the entire potato. Plant celery between the potato rows.

**Earthing up potatoes** When the plant height is about 8" (20 cm), earth up for the first time, then again after another two weeks.

**Adding fertilizer** Add a handful of fermented organic fertilizer a month after planting celery. The plants will grow tall and healthy if you keep adding fertilizer every three weeks.

**Harvesting** Dig up the potatoes once the part above the ground is dead. Potato may be damaged if temperatures have been cold for a while. Harvest celery after the plant reaches 12" (30 cm) in height. You can either harvest the whole plant or pick the outer leaves.

## TIP

If the soil dries out easily, lay straw mulch around the celery. In addition, if you want tender celery stems, cover the stock with cardboard or similar.

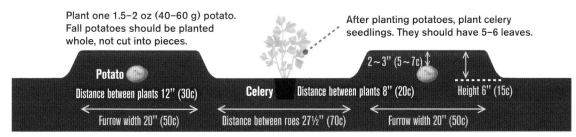

Plant one 1.5–2 oz (40–60 g) potato. Fall potatoes should be planted whole, not cut into pieces.

After planting potatoes, plant celery seedlings. They should have 5–6 leaves.

Potato — Distance between plants 12" (30c)

Celery — Distance between plants 8" (20c)

2~3" (5~7c)   Height 6" (15c)

Furrow width 20" (50c)   Distance between roes 27½" (70c)   Furrow width 20" (50c)

## Let's look at the effects

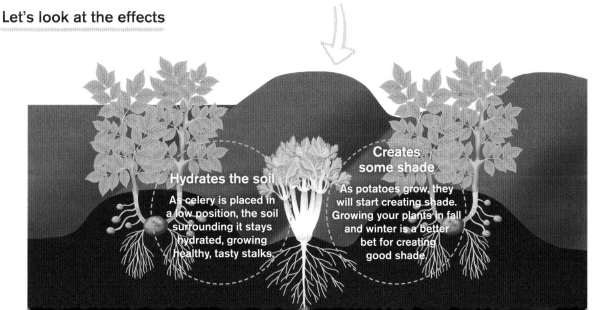

**Hydrates the soil**
As celery is placed in a low position, the soil surrounding it stays hydrated, growing healthy, tasty stalks.

**Creates some shade**
As potatoes grow, they will start creating shade. Growing your plants in fall and winter is a better bet for creating good shade.

# Taro & Ginger

Speeds up growth    Efficient use of space

## Increase the size of harvest by cultivating two types of plants that like water

Taro and ginger both originate in tropical areas of Asia where the temperature is as high as 77–86 degrees Fahrenheit (25–30 degrees Celsius), so they both prefer places with a lot of water. As the cultivation period is almost the same, you can grow them together in the same furrow.

During the hot and humid rainy season, taro grows big leaves and creates shade around it. If planted on the east and west side of the taro furrow, ginger can grow well in the shade created by the taro leaves.

If you have furrows that go from south to north, it is recommended to grow ginger between taro seedlings that aren't spaced too far apart. Taro and ginger will not compete for nutrients; rather, they will enhance each other's growth.

### CULTIVATION PROCESS

**Selecting varieties** Any variety will work for both plants.

**Mixing soil** Prepare a furrow three weeks before planting. Though both plants grow well without much fertilizer, you can add mature compost or fermented organic fertilizer if necessary.

**Planting** The appropriate period is mid April to mid May. Plant taro and cover the top with 2–3" (5–7 cm) of soil. If you "plant upside down" (sprouting side down, it) will grow vigorously and yield a bigger harvest. Ginger is planted between taro plants. Break seed ginger by hand into pieces of about 1.75 oz (50 g) and plant three at a time.

**Adding fertilizer, earthing up** Three months after taro stems have sprouted, add rice bran or fermented organic fertilizer and mix gently. Do this again after another month. Earth up for the first time from late May to mid June and again one month later. To prevent the soil from drying after the rainy season, cover the furrow with straw and moisturize it early. In the case of "upside-down planting," no earthing up is required.

**Harvesting** Both taro and ginger are harvested before the frost in early to mid November.

### TIP

You can pick leaves and bits of the ginger rhizome as early as four months after planting. If you harvest your ginger early, you can still continue to grow taro to maturity.

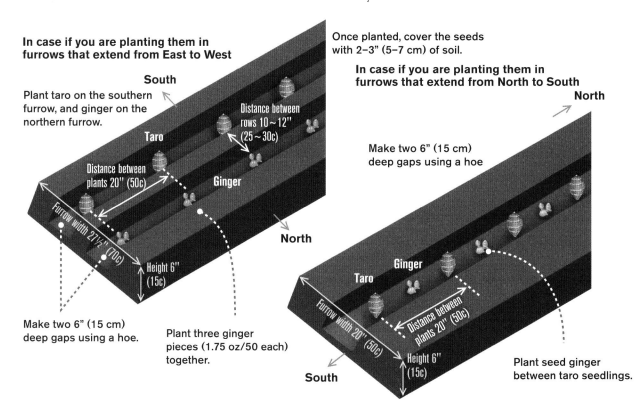

**In case if you are planting them in furrows that extend from East to West**

South

Plant taro on the southern furrow, and ginger on the northern furrow.

Taro

Distance between rows 10~12" (25~30c)

Ginger

Distance between plants 20" (50c)

Furrow width 27½" (70c)

Height 6" (15c)

North

Make two 6" (15 cm) deep gaps using a hoe.

Plant three ginger pieces (1.75 oz/50 each) together.

Once planted, cover the seeds with 2–3" (5–7 cm) of soil.

**In case if you are planting them in furrows that extend from North to South**

North

Make two 6" (15 cm) deep gaps using a hoe

Ginger

Taro

Furrow width 20" (50c)

Distance between plants 20" (50c)

Height 6" (15c)

South

Plant seed ginger between taro seedlings.

# Let's look at the effects

**Creates shade for ginger**

Ginger grows well even in summer when it grows under the shade of the taro leaves. The shade helps the soil stay hydrated.

Taro

Ginger

As roots of both plants do not grow too long, they will not be competing for nutrients in the soil.

Both plants grow edible roots well, thus increasing the size of the harvest.

# Taro & Daikon

Efficient use of space   Speeds up growth

## Grow rare summer-planted daikon in the shade of taro leaves

Daikon can be planted in late March to early April and harvested in June to July. Alternatively, you can plant daikon from late August to late September, and harvest it from late October to February next year. The optimal temperature for daikon cultivation is around 68 degrees Fahrenheit (20 degrees Celsius), with growth slowing down when temperatures reach about 77 degrees (25 degrees Celsius). Warmer temperatures also bring on more pests.

Using the shade of taro leaves, you can make a cool environment for growing daikon in summer. If you plant daikon seeds in mid-June to mid-July when taro is earthed up for the second time, taro will have spread large leaves to create proper shade. By mid-August to mid-September, you can harvest healthy daikon.

### CULTIVATION PROCESS

**Selecting varieties** Any variety will work for taro. For daikon, use one that is immune to disease-causing pests that can affect the plant during the time of cultivation.

**Mixing soil** Prepare a furrow three weeks before planting taro. Though it grows well without fertilizer, add mature compost or fermented organic fertilizer if necessary.

**Planting of taro** The appropriate period is mid April to mid May. Plant and cover it with about 2–3" (5–7 cm) of soil. If you "plant upside down" (sprouting side down), it will grow vigorously and yield a bigger harvest.

**Adding fertilizer to taro, earthing up** See p. 84.

**Planting daikon** Sow seeds between taro stocks between mid-July and mid-July. Cover the furrow with straw mulch so that the soil does not dry out after the rainy season.

**Thinning daikon** Thin daikon sprouts to three plants per spot when there is one leaf, grow two plants per spot when there are 3–4 leaves, and grow one per spot when there are 6–7 leaves.

**Harvesting** Harvest daikon 60–70 days after planting seeds. If you leave it for too long, the roots may crack or become diseased. Harvest taro in the first half of November before the frost hits.

### TIP

In the furrow that extends from east to west, plant daikon seeds on the north side to grow in the shade created by the taro. In a furrow that extends from north to south, plant the seeds on the east side between taro stocks to avoid the west sun.

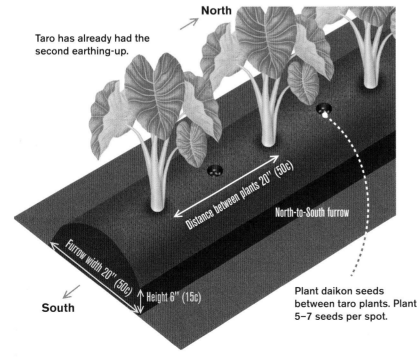

North

Taro has already had the second earthing-up.

Distance between plants 20" (50c)

North-to-South furrow

Furrow width 20" (50c)

Height 6" (15c)

South

Plant daikon seeds between taro plants. Plant 5–7 seeds per spot.

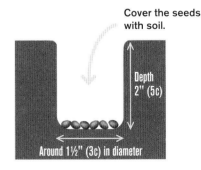

**Planting daikon seeds**

Cover the seeds with soil.

Depth 2" (5c)

Around 1½" (3c) in diameter

# Taro & Celery

## Grow branching vegetables while also repelling pests

If you grow celery on its own on the furrow, the seedling will grow hard green stalks and tough leaves. The trick to growing delicious celery is to slightly suppress its growth by limiting the light it receives and avoiding dehydration. Many farmers who produce and sell celery often cover the leaves and stalks with cardboard boxes to maintain optimum taste.

An easy way to accomplish this is by growing celery between taro seedlings that will ultimately create shade. The method is the same as for growing taro and daikon (see p. 86)—taro leaves that have grown large will create shade to allow celery to grow tasty stalks and leaves.

As with other Umbelliferae plants, celery has a unique scent that repels pests that are attracted to taro. **Application** You can also use parsley instead of celery. As parsley also likes a little bit of shade, you can grow high quality parsley leaves that are not bitter or hard if pared with taro.

## CULTIVATION PROCESS

**Selecting varieties** Any variety can work for both plants.

**Mixing soil** See p. 84.

**Planting of taro** See p. 84.

**Adding fertilizer of taro, earthing up** See p. 84.

**Planting celery, seeding** Plant celery in mid-July to mid-August, after earthing up taro. Plant celery between taro plants. Commercial seedlings can be used, but when raising seedlings, put the seeds in water for a whole day, anytime from the end of May to the beginning of June, wrap them in damp gauze or dishcloth, and place them in a cool shade to promote rooting. When the seedling has about three leaves, it's ready to go into the ground.

**Straw mulching** After planting celery, lay straw mulch to retain moisture.

**Harvesting** Harvest celery when it is over 12" (30 cm) in plant height. Cut at the bottom of the stock and harvest with the stock, or scrape from the outer leaves. The taro is harvested before frost in early to mid November.

## TIP

Lighter stalks are more tender, darker ones tend to have more nutrients.

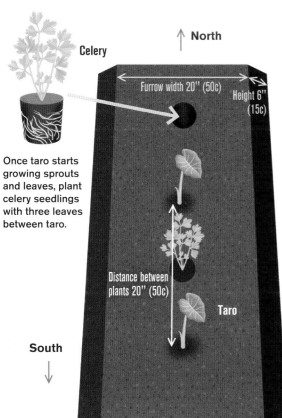

Celery

↑ North

Furrow width 20" (50c)

Height 6" (15c)

Once taro starts growing sprouts and leaves, plant celery seedlings with three leaves between taro.

Distance between plants 20" (50c)

Taro

South ↓

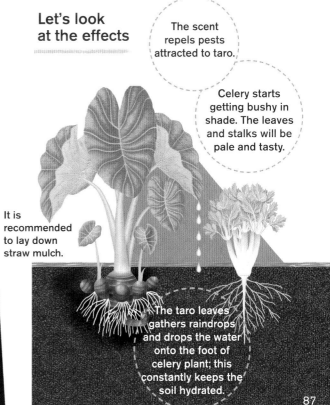

**Let's look at the effects**

The scent repels pests attracted to taro.

Celery starts getting bushy in shade. The leaves and stalks will be pale and tasty.

It is recommended to lay down straw mulch.

The taro leaves gathers raindrops and drops the water onto the foot of celery plant; this constantly keeps the soil hydrated.

# Strawberry & Garlic

Speeds up growth

Prevents disease

Repels pests

Efficient use of space

## Lengthen the cultivation of strawberries and increase the size of harvest

If you plant garlic near strawberries, strawberry seedlings will grow slightly tall, having been given just enough stress. Upon sprouting, strawberries go through phases, converting nutrients to plant matter, maturation, producing runners (stolons). Pairing strawberries with garlic accelerates flowering by 1–2 weeks. This results in more flowers and a bigger harvest.

Allicin, the chemical compound that gives garlic its scent, also has a bactericidal effect. Furthermore, the root releases antibiotic microorganisms, shielding strawberries from diseases. As strawberries rarely have plant lice, which carry viral infections, this cultivation method will also be beneficial to other plants that will be grown later. See p. 89 for cultivation technique.

**Application** You can also use scallions instead of garlic.

### CULTIVATION PROCESS

**Selecting varieties** Any variety will work for both plants.

**Mixing soil** Three weeks before planting, add fully matured compost and fermented organic fertilizer to prepare.

**Planting** Plant strawberry seedlings in mid-September to late October. Plant garlic between strawberry plants.

**Adding fertilizer** Add fermented organic fertilizer once in early November and again in late February.

**Harvesting** As garlic starts growing flower spikes in April, trim it down and use the stems (scapes), which are delicious and can be prepared in lots of ways. You can keep harvesting strawberries from early May to mid-June. Dig up the garlic when 80% of the portion above ground is dead.

### TIP

Strawberries grow runners one after another after harvest. Transplant the child stock in a pot and fix it in place with a wire or similar. You can prepare seedlings for the next season. As the first offspring may have inherited disease from the parent, use the second or third seedlings. If you plant green onion where garlic is dug up, it will have the same protective properties of the garlic.

## Let's look at the effects

Garlic

Strawberry

Allicin, a chemical compound responsible for the smell of garlic, has bactericidal effects.

A healthly level of competition allows flowers to bloom and develop fruits 1–2 weeks earlier.

The scent of garlic repels lice.

The strawberry plant grows bushy. The good air circulation helps prevent disease.

You can decrease the number of antagonistic bacteria by means of microorganism living on the garlic roots.

# Strawberry & Petunia

## Increase the possibility of bearing fruits by attracting insects that can help pollinate the flowers

Strawberries sometimes bear oddly shaped fruits. This happens when the fruit wasn't pollinated properly. In order to pollinate the flowers properly and grow high quality strawberries, various methods are used to attract pollinating insects to the plot.

Flower-visiting insects are drawn by the scent or sight of the flowers. Petunia grows in various vibrant colors and flowers bloom continuously during the time when strawberries are also in flower—two insect-attracting flowers in one place.

**Application** In place of petunia, you can also grow any type of flowering plants whose flowers bloom in spring and attract insects.

### CULTIVATION PROCESS

**Selecting varieties** Any variety will work for strawberry. It is convenient to use store-bought petunia seedlings. If you would like to grow petunia from seed, plant in September to October, and help it survive the winter by keeping the plant hydrated.

**Mixing soil** See p. 88

**Cultivating strawberry** See p. 88

**Planting petunias** Scatter seeds across the strawberry furrow. Though petunia sometimes dies from cold wind or frost, it is surprisingly strong when planted behind strawberry.

**Harvesting** See p. 88

### TIP

Pungent herbs are good companions for strawberries, repelling the pests to which strawberry is susceptible. Coriander, sage and mint are just a few options. Remember to grow the more invasive herbs in containers rather than in the ground.

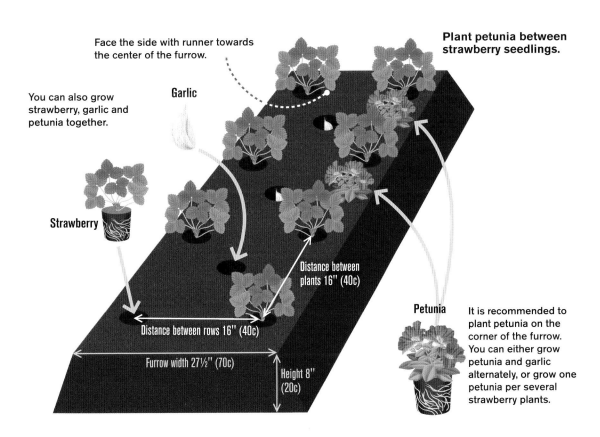

Face the side with runner towards the center of the furrow.

**Plant petunia between strawberry seedlings.**

You can also grow strawberry, garlic and petunia together.

Garlic

Strawberry

Distance between plants 16" (40c)

Distance between rows 16" (40c)

Furrow width 27½" (70c)

Height 8" (20c)

Petunia

It is recommended to plant petunia on the corner of the furrow. You can either grow petunia and garlic alternately, or grow one petunia per several strawberry plants.

# Red Perilla & Green Perilla

## Repel each other's pests by using different colors and scents

While both red perilla and green perilla originate from the same plant and are quite similar, when you eat them you notice that they have a slightly different taste and scent. They are also used for different purposes when cooked. Strangely enough, red perilla and green perilla have different types of pests. This has not been scientifically explained, but this is probably because pests sort their preferences according to the smell and taste of the plants. Therefore, growing red and green perilla is beneficial because you can minimize pest damage to both of them.

One thing to beware of is that, as they are quite similar in terms of plant type, when they have flowers it is quite common for them to pollinate each other. If you plant the seeds resulting from this pairing, you may encounter perilla plants with mixed, dirty-looking leaves with little scent. If you wish to grow perilla for its seeds, it is better to grow each plant on its own.

### CULTIVATION PROCESS

**Selecting varieties** Any variety will work for both plants.

**Raising seedlings** Make a shallow gap in the nursery box, and plant seeds every ½" (1 cm). Lightly cover the seeds with soil.

**Mixing soil** Three weeks before planting, add mature compost and fermented organic fertilizer to prepare a furrow.

**Planting** Plant the seedlings when they have grown six leaves. It is better to grow them next to each other, 24" (60 cm) between rows.

**Adding fertilizer, straw mulch** When the plant height is 8" (20 cm), apply fermented organic fertilizer or dregs. In order to protect from summer dryness, lay down straw mulch at the foot the stock.

**Harvesting** You can harvest the lower leaves from plants that have ten or more. It grows poorly if you harvest the soft leaves near the top. There is also a method involving nipping the top part with 7–8 leaves and growing the side shoots. This makes it feasible to keep harvesting soft leaves little by little.

### TIP

In addition to leaves, you can pick flower spikes to use, or harvest them as "fruits of perilla." Be careful, because the seeds are easy to spill and weed.

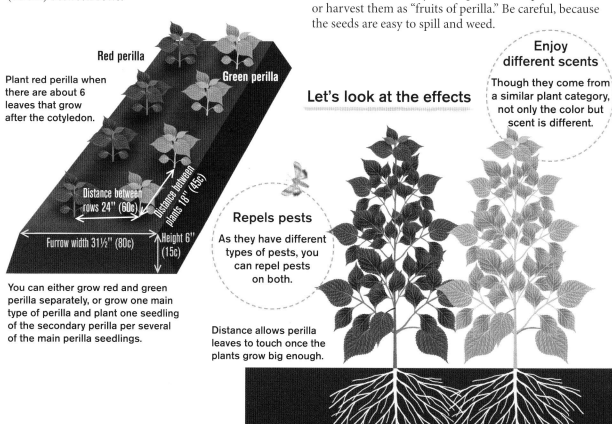

**Red perilla**

**Green perilla**

Plant red perilla when there are about 6 leaves that grow after the cotyledon.

Distance between rows 24" (60c)

Distance between plants 18" (45c)

Furrow width 31½" (80c)

Height 6" (15c)

You can either grow red and green perilla separately, or grow one main type of perilla and plant one seedling of the secondary perilla per several of the main perilla seedlings.

**Let's look at the effects**

**Enjoy different scents**

Though they come from a similar plant category, not only the color but scent is different.

**Repels pests**

As they have different types of pests, you can repel pests on both.

Distance allows perilla leaves to touch once the plants grow big enough.

# Myoga Ginger & Rosemary

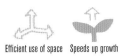

Efficient use of space    Speeds up growth

## A destructionist-type plant, rosemary somehow allows only myoga ginger to grow

Rosemary is a highly aromatic plant of the Labiatae family. You can harvest the soft leaves on the tip of the stem to use as herbs. It grows into a bush if you grow it for several years. However, as its strong scent affects other plants, few plants can grow near the foot of rosemary.

One of the plants that tolerates such proximity to rosemary is myoga ginger. When these plants are paired, it's as if nothing will stop the growth of either. This is a strange phenomenon not yet scientifically explained; however, this allows you to use the space efficiently and grow a different type of plant. You could say this combination teaches you one of the basics of companion planting.

## CULTIVATION PROCESS

**Selecting varieties** Any variety will work for both plants.

**Mixing soil** Choose a sunny place with good drainage and ventilation. Till the soil at least a week before planting. If it is a sterile plot, you may apply mature compost and fermented organic fertilizer.

**Cultivating rosemary** Use purchased seedlings, or cut the tip of a rosemary branch that has already grown to app. 3" (7–8 cm) to create seedlings. You can plant in 2–3 weeks. The appropriate planting period is from April to June. When the branch extends to about 8" (20 cm), turn the tip back. The side shoots will grow, so prune them as they grow.

**Cultivating myoga ginger** Planting period is mid-March to early April. Plant myoga ginger about 8" (20 cm) away from the already-planted rosemary. As it likes places with some shade, find a place that does not get the direct sunlight of midsummer.

**Adding fertilizer** Both plants grow well without added fertilizer.

**Straw mulching** Rosemary prefers a well-drained area, but myoga ginger hates dryness. If the soil dries out easily, spread straw mulch around myoga ginger.

**Harvesting** Cut and use the tip of the soft, newly grown rosemary branch. Harvest myoga ginger buds in fall during the first year, or in summer after the second year.

## TIP

Rosemary grows gradually, so after about three years, dig up myoga ginger and replant the plants slightly further away from the rosemary plant.

## Let's look at the effects

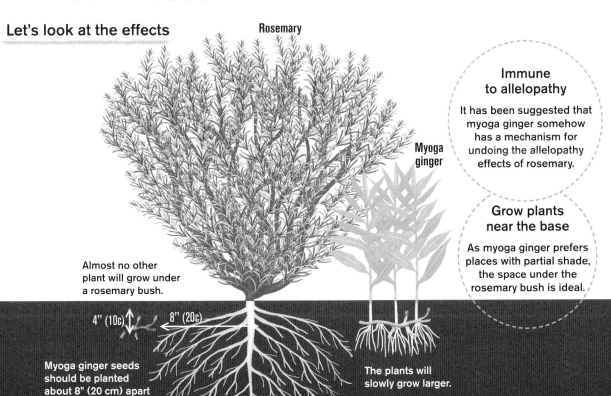

Rosemary

Myoga ginger

**Immune to allelopathy**

It has been suggested that myoga ginger somehow has a mechanism for undoing the allelopathy effects of rosemary.

**Grow plants near the base**

As myoga ginger prefers places with partial shade, the space under the rosemary bush is ideal.

Almost no other plant will grow under a rosemary bush.

4" (10c)    8" (20c)

Myoga ginger seeds should be planted about 8" (20 cm) apart from each other.

The plants will slowly grow larger.

column 3

# Tips on How to Use Banker Plants, Barrier Crops and Border Crops

One means of organizing your plot and allowing plants to grow well is using banker plants, barrier crops or border crops. These also fall under the realm of "companion plants." Though many of the examples below are more suited to small farming, gardeners can benefit from pairing protective plants with their crops.

## From attracting beneficial insects, repelling pests, to deterring animals, to providing protection from the wind

Dent corn, sorghum, vetiver, sunflower, crotalaria, oats, green locust, marigolds, cosmos, and so on are all highly active, and natural enemies such as arachnids, mantis, ladybugs, lacewings and others feed on insect pests that occur on these crops.

Planting dent corn, sorgo, vetiver, sunflower, crotalaria, etc., which grow taller as they fill their space on the plot, will function as a barrier to prevent the entry of pests from the outside. Planting windward and leeward will also shield plants from strong winds. Herbs such as rosemary and lavender can also be used as border crops. At the same time, they attract flower-visiting insects such as bees and help pollinate cucumbers, pumpkins, okra and strawberries while using their unique smells to repel pests.

There are also plants that can be used to deter harmful animals. For example, planting cluster amaryllis, narcissus, and so on as a border crop is effective, as these have toxic substances in their bulbs, thus preventing the invasion of moles and and other garden pests.

## Type of banker plants and their expected outcomes

| Banker plant | Expected outcome |
|---|---|
| Red clover | Increases the mycoparasites that can kill powdery mildew |
| Oat | Increases beneficial insects by many |
| Chinese plantain | Increases the mycoparasites that can kill powdery mildew |
| Pink wood sorrel | Increases natural enemies of spider mites |
| Wood sorrel | Increases natural enemies of spider mites |
| Common vetch | Increase natural enemies of plant lice and spider mites |
| Sorrel | Increase natural enemies of handsome fungus beetle (spotted lady bug) |
| Hemerocallis | Increase natural enemies of scale insects |
| Nasturtium | Increase natural enemies of pests such as plant lice, spider mites and thrips |
| Crimson clover | Increase natural enemies of thrips and plant lice |
| Cosmos | Increase natural enemies by many. Also attracts flower-visiting insects |
| White clover | Increase natural enemies of armyworm |
| Sorgo | Increases natural enemies by many. |
| Wheats | Increases natural enemies by many. Also increases mycoparasites that can kill powdery mildew. |
| Marigold | Increases natural enemies by many. Attracts flower visiting insects |
| Rattlebox | Increases natural enemies by many |
| Sunflower | Increases natural enemies by many. Also attracts flower visiting insects |
| Mugwort | Increases natural enemies of plant lice, spider mites and thrips. |
| Corn | Increases natural enemies by many |
| Dent corn | Increases natural enemies by many |
| Lavender | Increases natural enemies by many. Also attracts flower visiting insects. |
| Rosemary | Increases natural enemies by many. Also attracts flower visiting insects. |
| Berries | Increases natural enemies by many |

## Examples of banker plants and barrier crops

**Green pepper & sorgo**
Example of planting sorgo as a barrier next to green pepper. Sorgo prevents pests from invading from the outside, and at the same time, becomes a habitat for beneficial insects that can prevent pest damage.

**Pumpkin & dent corn**
In an open area, using dent corn as a shield from the wind is effective. As it has a longer cultivation period than sweetcorn, it can function as a barrier for a longer period of time.

**Chinese cabbage & oat**
Example of growing oats on the walkways between the Chinese cabbage furrows. Oats become a habitat for beneficial insects, which can minimize pest damage. It can also reduce the risk of clubroot.

## ● Banker planting with oat

### Becomes a habitat for beneficial insects
Though it will attract pests, it will also attract natural enemies that eat the pests on vegetables.

### Hydrates soil
As the leaves spread to create shade on the soil, the soil is kept moist.

### Prevent diseases on Brassicaceae plants
Avenacin (similar to saponin), a bactericidal substance, is released from oat. It can prevent clubroot on Brassicaceae plants.

### Also usable as green manure
By fall, oats will die and the dead leaves and stems cover the ground. As there will also be a lot of roots, it is possible to provide plenty of raw organic substance at once. Useful for mixing soil.

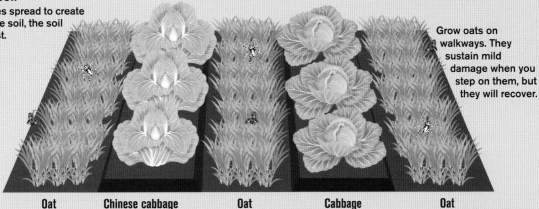

Grow oats on walkways. They sustain mild damage when you step on them, but they will recover.

Oat     Chinese cabbage     Oat     Cabbage     Oat

## ● Barrier planting with sorgo

### Plant 3–4 rows
You can even surround your entire plot.

### Works as blinds for pests
As the plants are tall, stink bugs, scarab beetles, and armyworms can't find the vegetables hiding behind sorgo.

### Becomes a habitat to natural enemies
Pests show up, but natural enemies will also be attracted.

### Functions as a windshield
If you plant sorgo upwind/downwind, you can protect your vegetables from strong winds.

### Also usable as green manure
If you mix the dead leaves and stems as they die, you can increase the amount of raw organic substance in the soil.

Upwind

As it creates some shade, vegetables that can grow in shade will grow well.

Plant eggplant far from the sorgo to make sure eggplant seedlings get the sunlight.

Downwind

Sorgo     Cabbage     Eggplant     Japanese mustard spinach     Sorgo

## ● Border planting with lavender

### Use it as pest repellent
Planting either upwind or downwind, the whole field is filled with the scent of lavender, which will serve as a pest repellent.

### Increases natural enemy
Lavender grows and becomes a habitat for beneficial insects that fight the pests on vegetables.

### Attracts flower visiting insects
Honeybees will be attracted to your plot. The bees can pollinate fruit flowers.

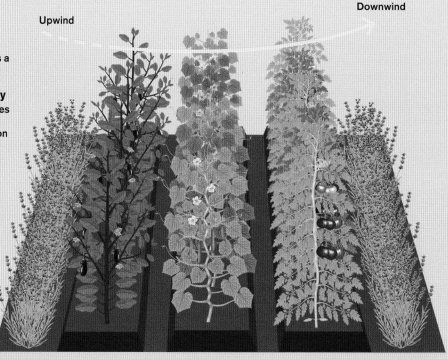

Upwind

Downwind

Lavender    Eggplant    Cucumber    Tomato    Lavender

## ● Framing with sunflowers

### Protects your crops from pests and winds
A row of tall sunflowers can be used as a barrier crop for insect and wind protection.

### The flower attracts beneficial insects as well as pests
Attracts flower-visiting insects, encouraging pollination of vegetables. Attracts enemies of pests like thrips and scarabs and reduces damage to vegetables.

### Dissolves phosphoric acid in the soil
The root dissolves insoluble phosphate in the soil, and has the ability to make other plants more capable of absorbing nutrients, which also helps reduce the need for fertilizer.

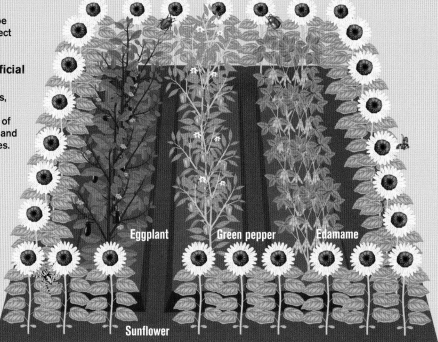

Eggplant    Green pepper    Edamame

Sunflower

# Companion Plants to Plant in Order

## Relay Planting

Here we will introduce some good combinations for growing
one plant after another. Depending on the combination, this can
provide several benefits such as eliminiating the necessity for
mixing soil, or preventing pest damage.

# Edamame & Chinese Cabbage

Speeds up growth

## Grow nutrient-absorbing plants after edamame enriches the soil

Edamame roots have root nodule bacteria, which capture nitrogen in the atmosphere and convert it to nutrients. Root nodule will break off from the roots after a certain period of time, and will bring rich nutrients to the soil. Therefore, any type of plants that are grown afterwards will grow well, but nutrient-absorbing Chinese cabbage is especially recommended.

If you plant edamame in late April to mid-May, you can harvest it by mid-June to August. Chinese cabbage absorbs the most nutrients right after being planted, and it will start growing sizable leaves if the first stage of growth goes well.

**Application** Instead of Chinese cabbage, you can plant any vegetable from the Brassicaceae plant family.

### CULTIVATION PROCESS

**Selecting varieties** Use early to middle varieties of edamame. Late varieties cannot be harvested by the planting time for Chinese cabbage. Any variety of Chinese cabbage will work.

**Cultivating edamame** See p. 42–45. When harvesting, cut the plant from the base and leave the roots. Stems and leaves can be left on the soil as mulch.

**Mixing soil during relay** After harvesting the edamame, mix the roots and residue and build a furrow. Because summer temperatures are high, roots and residue break down in about two weeks, and the soil's microflora stabilizes, but it is safer to wait for three weeks before planting Chinese cabbage.

**Planting Chinese cabbage** Plant seeds in plastic pots by late August. Plant seedlings from mid to late September.

**Adding fertilizer** Check the growth of the cabbage's outer leaves; if necessary, add fertilizer, such as fermented organic fertilizer.

**Harvest** Edamame is harvested when beans are fully developed in the pods. If the Chinese cabbage feels firm when pressed, harvest it from the stock source.

### TIP

Chinese cabbage grows well because the roots and residue of edamame are decomposed into nitrate nitrogen. Cabbage can absorb even relatively raw organic matter, so even if the roots of edamame are left in the soil, it will grow sufficiently even if they are planted without tilling.

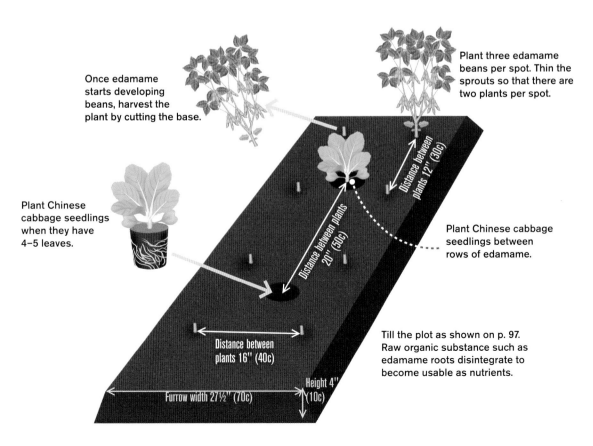

Once edamame starts developing beans, harvest the plant by cutting the base.

Plant three edamame beans per spot. Thin the sprouts so that there are two plants per spot.

Plant Chinese cabbage seedlings when they have 4–5 leaves.

Distance between plants 12" (30c)

Distance between plants 20" (50c)

Plant Chinese cabbage seedlings between rows of edamame.

Distance between plants 16" (40c)

Furrow width 27½" (70c)

Height 4" (10c)

Till the plot as shown on p. 97. Raw organic substance such as edamame roots disintegrate to become usable as nutrients.

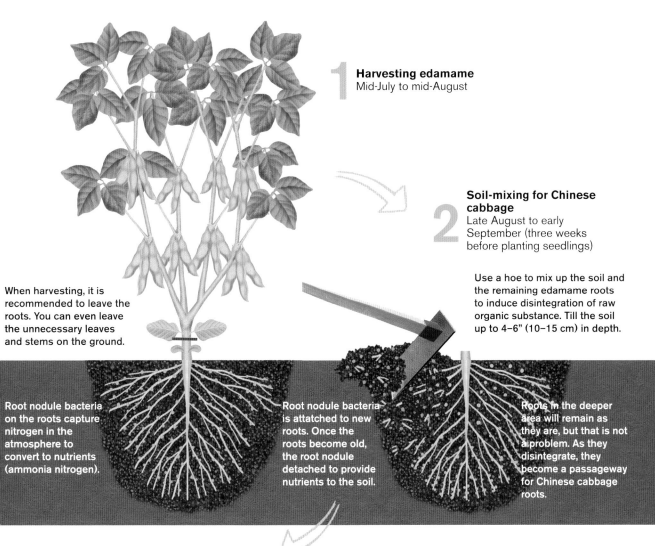

## 1 Harvesting edamame
Mid-July to mid-August

## 2 Soil-mixing for Chinese cabbage
Late August to early September (three weeks before planting seedlings)

Use a hoe to mix up the soil and the remaining edamame roots to induce disintegration of raw organic substance. Till the soil up to 4–6" (10–15 cm) in depth.

When harvesting, it is recommended to leave the roots. You can even leave the unnecessary leaves and stems on the ground.

Root nodule bacteria on the roots capture nitrogen in the atmosphere to convert to nutrients (ammonia nitrogen).

Root nodule bacteria is attached to new roots. Once the roots become old, the root nodule detached to provide nutrients to the soil.

Roots in the deeper area will remain as they are, but that is not a problem. As they disintegrate, they become a passageway for Chinese cabbage roots.

## 4 Harvesting Chinese cabbage
From late November

Chinese cabbage develops a solid head if large outer leaves photosynthesize to create a lot of leaves.

Raw organic substance is broken down into nutrients for Chinese cabbage.

## 3 Planting Chinese cabbage
Mid-September to late September

If the growth of outer leaves is poor, add fermented organic fertilizer around the plant in mid-October and early November.

Microorganisms suddenly increase in number and start disintegrating raw organic substance like edamame roots. In 2–3 weeks, most of it will be disintegrated and microorganisms become less active. This is the best environment for Chinese cabbage to receive plenty of nutrients.

# Edamame & Carrots, Daikon

Speeds up growth

## Relay the cultivation without adding fertilizer. Root vegetables grow without damage to the skin

Root vegetables like carrots and daikon have great chemistry with edamame, and this relay planting has long been practiced by farmers.

Both carrots and daikon grow well without much fertilizer. They still require soil-mixing practices like tilling. If you add too much fertilizer to the soil at this stage, there will be some raw microorganisms and undisintegrated fertilizer remaining in the soil. This will damage the surface of the roots.

If you reuse the space that was previously used to grow edamame, the root nodule bacteria will enrich the soil, making fertilizing unnecessary. If you harvest edamame from the roots and plant carrot or daikon seeds, they will grow smoothly. You can harvest high quality carrots or daikon using this method.

**Application** You can also use other root vegetables like greater burdock.

## CULTIVATION PROCESS

**Selecting varieties** Select early-medium to mid-season varieties of edamame. Choose smaller carrot varieties. It is hard to relay plant deep-rooted ones planted in summer. Daikon can be of any variety.

**Cultivating edamame** See p. 42–45. Dig up roots at harvest time.

**Mixing soil during the relay** After harvesting edamame, cultivate without applying compost or manure. Till the soil deeply where daikon will be planted.

**Growing carrots and daikon** Plant seeds about three weeks after mixing the soil. Plant carrots seeds in a shallow ditch and cover thinly, and then tamp down to make the seeds and soil adhere tightly. Plant 5–7 daikon seeds per spot.

**Thinning** Thin carrot so that there are 2–2½" (5–6 cm) between plants at a plant height of 1½–2" (4–5 cm).

When the root is about ¼" (5 mm) in diameter, thin it to 4–5" (10–12 cm) between stocks. Thin daikon so there are three plants per spot at one leaf, two at 3–4 leaves, and only one plant per spot at 6–7 leaves.

**Adding fertilizer** Not necessary.

**Harvesting** Harvest from the roots that are thick enough. Harvest daikon by the end of January. Carrots can be harvested until the beginning of March.

## TIP

Daikon is Brassicaceae, carrots are Umbelliferae. Because they have different pests, pairing them has a pest repellent effect. Generally, carrots are planted in late July to mid-September, and daikon in late August to late September, but relay cultivation can start from late August. Carrots may be planted earlier, but if you plant it with daikon in early September, the repellent effect of pests will increase.

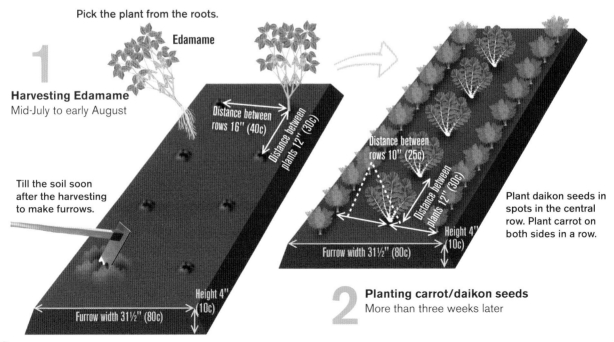

Pick the plant from the roots.

Edamame

**1**

**Harvesting Edamame**
Mid-July to early August

Till the soil soon after the harvesting to make furrows.

Distance between rows 16" (40c)

Distance between plants 12" (30c)

Height 4" (10c)

Furrow width 31½" (80c)

Distance between rows 10" (25c)

Distance between plants 12" (30c)

Height 4" (10c)

Furrow width 31½" (80c)

Plant daikon seeds in spots in the central row. Plant carrot on both sides in a row.

**2** **Planting carrot/daikon seeds**
More than three weeks later

# Watermelon & Spinach

Speeds up growth

## Grow deep-rooted plant after watermelon's deep roots develop the soil

Watermelon tends to grow deep roots Although it is native to hot, dry African deserts, its roots absorb water under the ground and its fruits are succulent.

Roots are like nature's rakes—when one plant grows deep roots, the plant grown afterwards is likely to do so as well. Here, we follow watermelon with spinach, which also grows deep roots. The remaining watermelon roots will disintegrate and become a path for air and water, helping to ensure that the spinich roots are healthy. As a result, spinach will have stronger immunity to diseases and will be delicious.
**Application** Instead of spinach, you can plant carrots, daikon, or greater burdock, all of which grow deep roots.

### CULTIVATION PROCESS

**Selecting varieties** Any variety will work for both plants.

**Cultivating Watermelon** See p. 32–33.

**Mixing soil at relay time** Watermelon's harvest period is from early to mid-August. After harvesting, organize the vines and leaves and apply mature compost and fermented organic fertilizer; lightly mix with the soil.

**Seeding of spinach** Plant seeds in a row three weeks after mixing the soil.

**Thinning, adding fertilizer** Spinach is thinned to 1–1½" (3–4 cm) between stocks with one true leaf, and to 2–3" (6–8 cm) between stocks at 2–2½" (5–6 cm) of plant height. When doing the second thinning, apply fermented organic fertilizer between the rows.

**Harvesting** If watermelon is planted in early to mid-May, you can harvest in mid-August. Spinach can be harvested when the plant height is 10–12" (25–30 cm).

### TIP

Watermelon furrow is generally high. After the harvest, even it out to a normal height, about 4" (10 cm) or slightly lower.

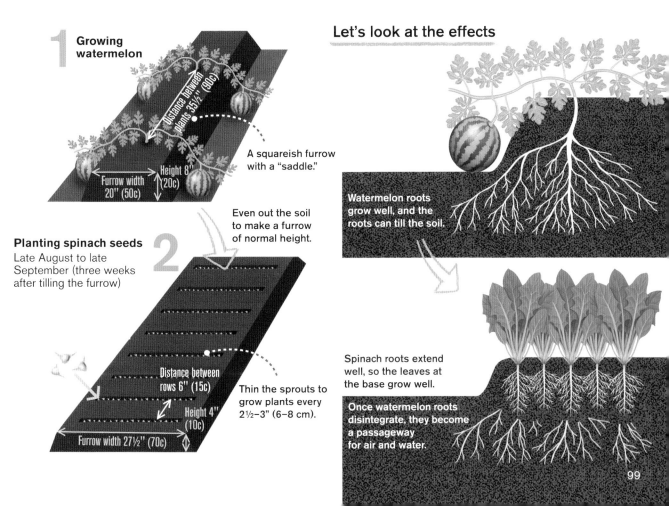

**1** Growing watermelon

Distance between plants 35½" (90c)

A squareish furrow with a "saddle."

Furrow width 20" (50c)  Height 8" (20c)

**Planting spinach seeds**
Late August to late September (three weeks after tilling the furrow)

**2**

Even out the soil to make a furrow of normal height.

Distance between rows 6" (15c)

Height 4" (10c)

Thin the sprouts to grow plants every 2½–3" (6–8 cm).

Furrow width 27½" (70c)

## Let's look at the effects

Watermelon roots grow well, and the roots can till the soil.

Spinach roots extend well, so the leaves at the base grow well.

Once watermelon roots disintegrate, they become a passageway for air and water.

99

# Tomatoes & Green Pak Choi

Repels pests  Speeds up growth

## Grow green pak choi from seeds with ease by preventing damage by cutworms

This is a method for growing fall-grown leafy vegetables after harvesting tomatoes in August. We recommend a Brassicaceae vegetable like green pak choi, which usually suffers the most damage from cutworms. Cutworm is the larva form of the turnip moth. It spends the daytime underground and damages the seedlings by night, returning above ground to eat the leaves.

Turnip moths lay eggs on vegetables or weeds near the ground; however, for some reason they avoid tomatoes. As tomatoes release strong scents that prevent other plants from growing nearby, weeds generally keep clear. By following tomatoes with pak choi, you provide the pak choi with a safer environment. **Application** You can also use Japanese mustard spinach, potherb mustard, turnip, crown daisy or spinach instead of green pak choi.

### CULTIVATION PROCESS

**Selecting varieties** Choose a tomato variety with larger fruits, which are often not grown until fall. Any variety will work for green pak choi.

**Tomato cultivation** See p. 14–15. As it becomes difficult to pollinate if it gets too hot, harvest the fruits until mid-August and clean up the stock.

**Mixing soil at relay time** Remove large roots, and till the soil to prepare a furrow. If the tomatoes didn't grow well, you may apply mature compost or fermented organic fertilizer.

**Seeding green pak choi** Plant seeds in early to late September, just over three weeks after mixing the soil. Plant 3–4 seeds per spot, or plant seeds in a row and thin the sprouts.

**Thinning, adding fertilizer** When seedlings have 1–2 leaves, thin and leave one per spot. If seeds were planted in a row, space seedlings at 2–2½" (5–6 cm) at 1–2 leaves, 4–5" (10–12 cm) at 3–4 leaves.

**Harvesting** Green pak choi is harvested when the bottom leaves are thick, usually 55–65 days after planting.

### TIP

Be careful, because green pak choi can suffer damage from the larvae of cabbage butterflies and moths if you start cultivating it too early.

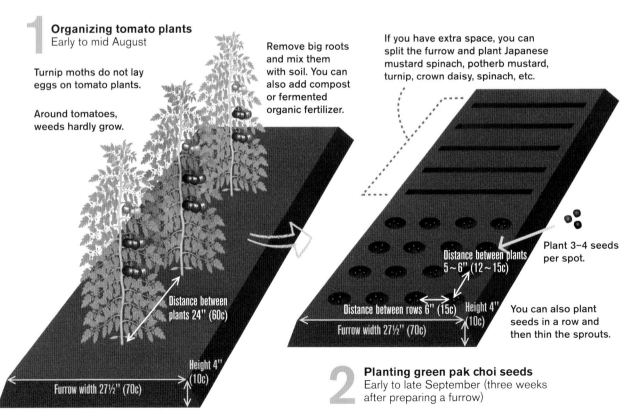

**1** **Organizing tomato plants**
Early to mid August

Turnip moths do not lay eggs on tomato plants.

Around tomatoes, weeds hardly grow.

Remove big roots and mix them with soil. You can also add compost or fermented organic fertilizer.

Distance between plants 24" (60c)

Height 4" (10c)

Furrow width 27½" (70c)

If you have extra space, you can split the furrow and plant Japanese mustard spinach, potherb mustard, turnip, crown daisy, spinach, etc.

Plant 3–4 seeds per spot.

Distance between plants 5~6" (12~15c)

Distance between rows 6" (15c)

Height 4" (10c)

Furrow width 27½" (70c)

You can also plant seeds in a row and then thin the sprouts.

**2** **Planting green pak choi seeds**
Early to late September (three weeks after preparing a furrow)

# Cucumbers & Garlic

## Diseases become rare when there are different types of rhizosphere microorganisms

Cucumbers usually spread shallow roots and require straw mulch when cultivating. Therefore, even after cucumber plants are harvested, it is common to have a lot of raw organic matter remaining in the soil.

A type of plant that can break down and benefit from raw organic matter is the Alliaceae family. Therefore, you can grow garlic after cucumbers because you can start planting in September to October. As cucumber is a dicotyledonous plant and garlic is a monocotyledonous plant, they have different types of microorganisms. Therefore, growing them one after another will not cause antagonistic bacteria to increase in number. You can also reduce the risk of diseases that commonly affect garlic, such as dry rot and spring rot.

**Application** You can also use Japanese leek, shallots or Japanese chive instead of garlic.

## CULTIVATION PROCESS

**Selecting varieties** Any variety will work for cucumber. For garlic, select a suitable variety for your region.

**Cucumber cultivation** See p. 24–27. Leaves will be damaged in August and growth will be sluggish, so finish the harvest from early to mid August and clean up the stock.

**Mixing soil during relay** Set up a furrow three weeks before planting garlic. If the cucumbers didn't grow well, add mature compost and fermented organic fertilizer before planting.

**Growing of garlic** Separate garlic pieces and plant one piece at a time. The depth is about 2–3" (5–8 cm).

**Adding fertilizer** When leaves grow to about 12" (30 cm), apply rice bran or fermented organic fertilizer to the area around it, and let it blend with the soil. Fertilize again after another month.

**Nipping** Flowering spikes grow in spring. Even if it does not affect the enlargement of garlic, it is better to cut back and use the stems.

**Harvesting** When about 80% of the portion above ground is dead, dig up on a sunny day. Cut the leaves and roots and dry them in the field for 2–3 days. Bundle them into bunches and store in a well-ventilated place.

## TIP

You may grow fall cucumber after garlic. Antibiotics from microorganismss that coexist on the roots of garlic reduce soil diseases such as cucumber scabs.

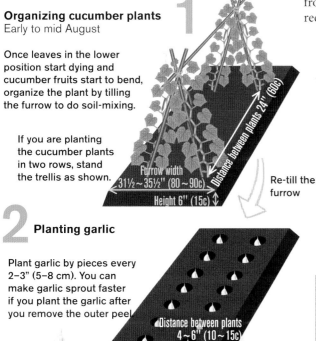

**Organizing cucumber plants**
Early to mid August

Once leaves in the lower position start dying and cucumber fruits start to bend, organize the plant by tilling the furrow to do soil-mixing.

If you are planting the cucumber plants in two rows, stand the trellis as shown.

Distance between plants 24" (60c)

Furrow width 31½ ~ 35½" (80 ~ 90c)

Height 6" (15c)

Re-till the furrow

**Planting garlic**

Plant garlic by pieces every 2–3" (5–8 cm). You can make garlic sprout faster if you plant the garlic after you remove the outer peel.

Distance between plants 4 ~ 6" (10 ~ 15c)

Distance between rows 12" (30c)

Height 4" (10c)

Furrow width 27½" (70c)

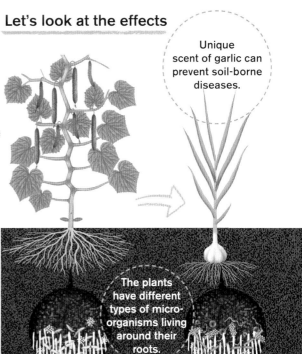

**Let's look at the effects**

Unique scent of garlic can prevent soil-borne diseases.

The plants have different types of micro-organisms living around their roots.

# Green Pepper & Spinach, Iceberg Lettuce

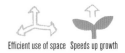

Efficient use of space    Speeds up growth

## Harvest vegetables mid-winter using green pepper as a shield from the cold

Similar to pairing eggplants and daikon (see p. 19), this is a method for utilizing the empty space around the foot of green pepper plants. Green pepper grows shallow roots and spreads wide, and may complete with other plants that grow shallow roots. Choose a companion that will grow deep roots. Smaller vegetables such as spinach or iceberg lettuce make better companions than larger vegetables such as daikon and cabbage.

Green pepper is fairly strong to cold. As long as it does not sustain severe frost damage, you can continue to harvest green pepper, as its leaves won't drop until the following January. Therefore, you can grow spinach or iceberg lettuce, which also handle cold well, in the fall. As pepper acts as a shield from wind and frost, you can harvest the vegetables in the middle of winter.

**Application** Instead of green pepper, you can grow sweet or red pepper. Instead of spinach or iceberg lettuce, tatsoi, leaf mustard, or wasabi can be grown, as they are also strong against the cold.

### CULTIVATION PROCESS

**Selecting varieties** Any varieties of peppers, spinach and iceberg lettuce will work.

**Pepper pepper cultivation** See p. 22–23.

**Planting spinach** By the end of August to the beginning of October. Plant seeds in a row and keep the distance between rows at 10–12" (25–30 cm).

**Planting iceberg lettuce** Plant around 10 to 12" (25–30 cm) apart between green pepper stocks from the end of August to the beginning of October.

**Adding fertilizer** It is good to apply a handful of fermented organic fertilizer to the green peppers once every 2–3 weeks until November. As spinach and lettuce utilize this fertilizer, there is no need fertilize them.

**Harvesting** Sweet peppers are harvested as they mature. They will wither in January. Both spinach and iceberg lettuce can be harvested until early February. Since lettuce is damaged when exposed to hard frost, it's good to place cheesecloth beforehand according to the weather.

### TIP

Even if there are relatively few remaining peppers to harvest in late fall, it is important to leave leaves and stems as long as possible. If it is a cold year and winter comes early, put cheesecloth or nonwoven fabric on the peppers. This sort of covering also works for spinach and iceberg lettuce as protection against cold.

**How to plant spinach seeds and iceberg lettuce**

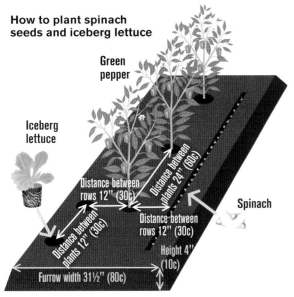

Green pepper

Iceberg lettuce

Distance between rows 12" (30c)

Distance between plants 24" (60c)

Distance between plants 12" (30c)

Distance between rows 12" (30c)

Spinach

Height 4" (10c)

Furrow width 31½" (80c)

Plant seeds in a line, ½" (1 cm) apart. Once there's a leaf after the cotyledon, thin the plants to a distance of 1–1½" (3–4 cm) between plants. Once they reach 2–2½" (5–6 cm) in height, thin again to a distance of 2½–3" (6–8 cm).

## Let's look at the effects

In January, leaves tend to become damaged; however, green pepper leaves will still shield spinach and lettuce from cold wind and frost.

Spinach spread leaves in a rosette shape in December. This will keep the soil hydrated for green pepper.

# Daikon & Cabbage

## Reduce the risk of clubroot and increase the chances of growing quality cabbage

One of the diseases that commonly affect cabbage is clubroot, a disease that only affects Brassicaceae plants. As the cultivation period for cabbage is long, and cabbage stops growing once it's affected by the disease, the damage is severe. The worst thing about clubroot is that the cells that cause it remain in the soil for a long time, so a five-year break before planting another Brassicaceae isn't effective enough. Surprisingly, you can rescue your cabbage by first growing another Brassicaceae—daikon. Although daikon can be affected by clubroot, the bacteria causing it will not increase, but will ultimately die out. In other words, daikon acts as a banker plant, cleaning out clubroot's antagonistic bacteria

**Application** You can also grow Chinese cabbage, broccoli, cauliflower, green pak choi, or turnip in place of cabbage.

### CULTIVATION PROCESS

**Selecting varieties** Although any variety will work, choosing a clubroot resistant (CR) cabbage variety is recommended if clubroot is a big problem in your garden.

**Daikon cultivation** See p. 72.

**Relay at the time of mixing soil** Three weeks before planting cabbage seedlings, lighten the leaves of the radish, and apply mature compost and fermented organic fertilizer to prepare a furrow.

**Planting cabbage** Plant when the seedlings have 4–5 leaves. Although it's common to space cabbages at about 20" (50 cm), you can plant more densely at about 12" (30 cm) to harvest a smaller head.

**Adding fertilizer, earthing up** About three weeks after planting cabbage, give a handful of fermented organic fertilizer to the soil. When the head starts forming, give the soil another handful.

**Harvesting** Dig up daikon at the appropriate time for each variety. If you leave it too long, it may crack. When cabbage starts forming heads, press the head and harvest if firm.

### TIP

If clubroot is a problem in your garden, you may want to plant cabbage seedlings in the pits vacated by the daikon. If necessary add some fertilizer near the plants. Another method for controlling clubroot is to densely plant leaf radish to thoroughly clean out the clubroot fungi.

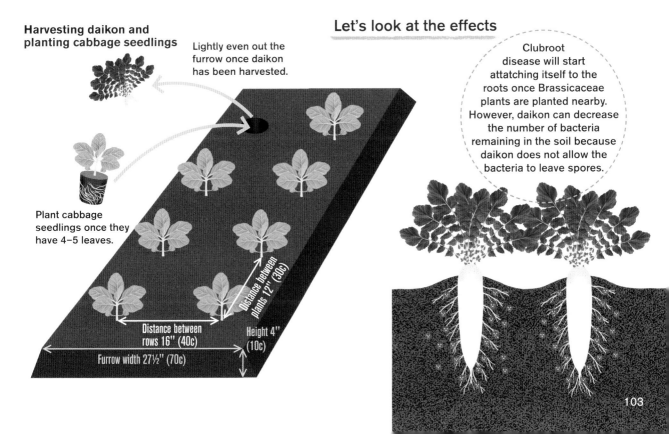

**Harvesting daikon and planting cabbage seedlings**

Lightly even out the furrow once daikon has been harvested.

Plant cabbage seedlings once they have 4–5 leaves.

Distance between plants 12" (30c)

Distance between rows 16" (40c)

Height 4" (10c)

Furrow width 27½" (70c)

## Let's look at the effects

Clubroot disease will start attatching itself to the roots once Brassicaceae plants are planted nearby. However, daikon can decrease the number of bacteria remaining in the soil because daikon does not allow the bacteria to leave spores.

103

# Daikon & Sweet Potatoes

Speeds up growth

## Improve the quality of vegetables by combining types of plants that grow well even in poor soil environment

When sweet potato plants are exposed to too much fertilizer, the vines overgrow, resulting in smaller sweet potatoes. It's best for sweet potatoes to follow a plant that won't leave too much fertilizer behind. As daikon doesn't require fertilizer, it's a good choice to precede sweet potatoes.

If you continue to grow these types of plants each year, daikon will grow smooth tubers that aren't overly bitter. Sweet potatoes won't overgrow their vines, but will instead yield big, tasty produce.

### CULTIVATION PROCESS

**Selecting varieties** Select daikon varieties suitable for spring planting to avoid bushiness. Any sweet potato variety will work.

**Daikon cultivation** See p. 72. Sowing is done from late March to early April.

**Mixing soil during relay** Set up the furrow without applying compost and manure after harvesting daikon.

**Sweet potato cultivation** See p. 78. Plant it by the end of July at the latest.

**Harvesting** Spring-sown daikon can be harvested in 70–80 days. If you miss the window, the daikon will grow too large, and may crack. Sweet potato is harvested between 110 and 120 days after planting. Harvest before the first frost hits

### TIP

In winter, decomposition of organic matter is slow. After digging up the sweet potato, cultivate it early to decompose the remaining organic matter, such as roots. Cultivate sweet potatoes early in areas where frost hits early. You can start the daikon early from the middle of March by using a plastic tunnel, a solid cover, or plastic mulch as needed.

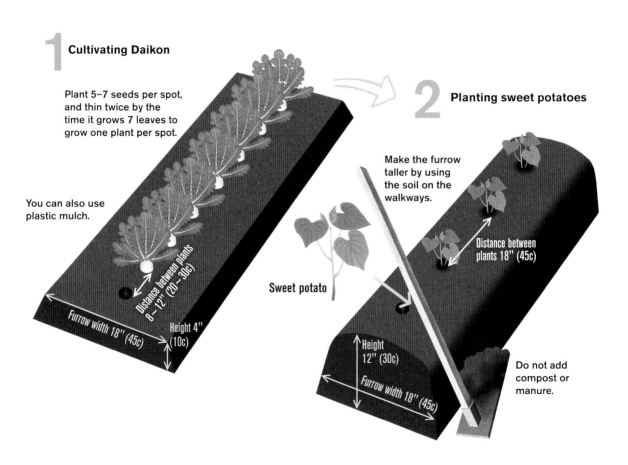

**1 Cultivating Daikon**

Plant 5–7 seeds per spot, and thin twice by the time it grows 7 leaves to grow one plant per spot.

You can also use plastic mulch.

Distance between plants 8 ~ 12" (20 ~ 30c)

Furrow width 18" (45c)

Height 4" (10c)

**2 Planting sweet potatoes**

Make the furrow taller by using the soil on the walkways.

Distance between plants 18" (45c)

Sweet potato

Height 12" (30c)

Furrow width 18" (45c)

Do not add compost or manure.

# Garlic & Okra

Speeds up growth   Prevents disease

## Grow okra well by using the remainder of garlic roots and fertilizers

Garlic grows relatively deep roots compared to other Fabaceae plants. When you harvest the garlic plant, the majority of the roots will remain in the soil as they break off from the harvested garlic root. In contrast, okra is a straight-rooted plant that will grow well if it's allowed to grow deep roots in the early stages of growth.

If you grow it after harvesting garlic, okra will use traces of garlic roots to grow deep roots. Also, as there will be plenty of raw organic substance and fertilizer left in the soil after the garlic harvest, you won't need to fertilize for okra. Okra will grow well even if you plant the seeds right after harvesting the garlic.

**Application** Just as in the case of onions on p. 106–107, you can also grow pumpkin, cucumber varieties that grow near the ground, fall-grown eggplants, or spinach after growing garlic.

### CULTIVATION PROCESS

**Selection of varieties** Any variety will work for both plants.

**Garlic cultivation** See p. 101.

**Mixing soil during relay** After harvesting garlic, use the furrow as it is. Compost and fertilizer aren't needed.

**Seeding okra** Okra grows deeper roots if you grow 3–4 plants per spot by planting 4–5 seeds per spot. When okra's growth is slow, it can be harvested without over-stretching or hardening.

**Adding fertilizer** Once the stems start to grow, apply a handful of fermented fertilizer once every three weeks.

**Harvesting** Okra is generally ready when the pods are 2–4" (5–10 cm) long.

### TIP

Since the appropriate time for sowing okra is from the beginning of May to the beginning of June, you may sow seeds before harvesting garlic by using the space between the garlic rows.

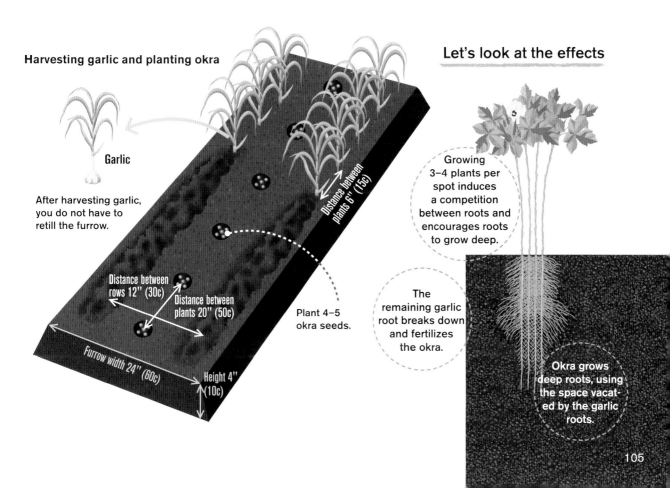

**Harvesting garlic and planting okra**

Garlic

After harvesting garlic, you do not have to retill the furrow.

Distance between plants 6" (15c)

Distance between rows 12" (30c)

Distance between plants 20" (50c)

Plant 4–5 okra seeds.

Furrow width 24" (60c)

Height 4" (10c)

**Let's look at the effects**

Growing 3–4 plants per spot induces a competition between roots and encourages roots to grow deep.

The remaining garlic root breaks down and fertilizes the okra.

Okra grows deep roots, using the space vacated by the garlic roots.

# Onions & Pumpkin

Prevents disease  Speeds up growth  Efficient use of space

## Cultivate using the remaining fertilizer

Although it depends on the plant species, the harvest season for onion is around May to June. You can grow pumpkin before the onion harvest.

As mentioned on p. 30, when pumpkin and scallions are planted so that their roots are touching, the antibiotic substance on the scallion roots can reduce the antagonistic bacteria for pumpkin. You can reduce the antagonistic bacteria before planting pumpkin if onions (also an Alliaceae plant) are grown beforehand. As onion cultivation often ends with rich soil, pumpkin will grow well without added fertilizer.

**Application** You can also apply this method to growing cucumbers or gourds.

### CULTIVATION PROCESS

**Selection of varieties** Any variety works for both. Early onion varieties allow more time for pumpkin cultivation.

**Onion cultivation** See p. 64–65. Bear in mind that pumpkins will need space for their vines to spread, so plan well in advance before growing your onions.

**Planting pumpkins** If you build a vinyl fence around the pumpkin stock until it has rooted, it will grow well, as it is protected from strong winds.

**Picking** When two or three side vines grow, pick up the tip of the parent vine.

**Adding fertilizer** Not needed.

**Harvesting** Harvest pumpkin about 50 days after the female flowers have bloomed. Be sure to bring them in before the first frost.

### TIP

Since the harvest time for onion is largely determined by the variety, grow or buy your pumpkin seedlings according to the resulting growing period. If the onion is an early variety, you can proceed to plant pumpkins without tilling the soil.

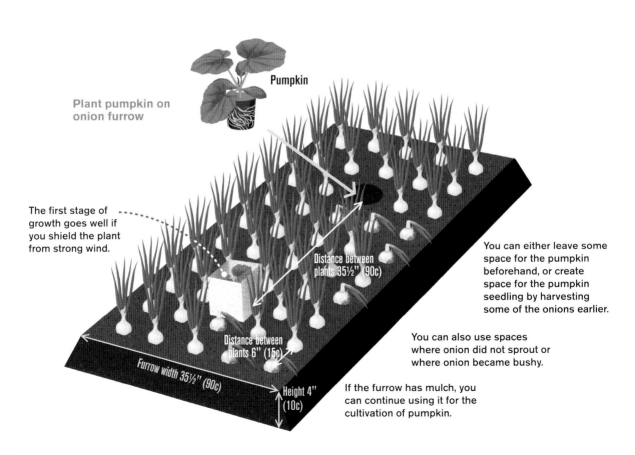

Pumpkin

Plant pumpkin on onion furrow

The first stage of growth goes well if you shield the plant from strong wind.

Distance between plants 35½" (90c)

Distance between plants 6" (15c)

Furrow width 35½" (90c)

Height 4" (10c)

You can either leave some space for the pumpkin beforehand, or create space for the pumpkin seedling by harvesting some of the onions earlier.

You can also use spaces where onion did not sprout or where onion became bushy.

If the furrow has mulch, you can continue using it for the cultivation of pumpkin.

# Onions & Fall Eggplant

Prevents disease    Speeds up growth

## Enjoy fall eggplant without worrying about disease

There are two ways to grow delicious eggplants in fall. Although it is common to keep harvesting eggplants from the seedlings planted in April to May, the plants start becoming stressed around summer. A solution to this problem is to prune the stems and cut the roots to give the plants some energy to grow fall-harvested eggplants.

Another way is to plant the seeds in early-to-mid May and seedlings in mid-to-late June, so that the seedlings can weather the summer while they are still young. In this case, you can have a smooth transition from harvesting onions to cultivating eggplants if you mix your soil immediately after harvesting onions.

As with planting pumpkin on p. 106, diseases aren't a concern, as onion roots release antibiotic bacteria that can kill the antagonistic bacteria.

**Application** Spinach is also a good choice to follow onions. As it can decrease the number of fusarium bacteria, you can prevent fusarium wilt.

## CULTIVATION PROCESS

**Selecting varieties** Any variety will work for both plants, but it is easier to use early to middle varieties of onions. Eggplants grow better with late varieties.

**Making soil during relay** After harvesting the onion, mix mature compost and fermented organic fertilizer with soil.

**Planting** Plant eggplant 2–3 weeks after mixing soil.

**Mulching** Eggplant doesn't like dehydration, so lay mulch such as straw mulch by mid July after the rainy season. You may also lay plastic mulch at the time of planting.

**Additional fertilization** For eggplant, apply a handful of fermented organic fertilizer to the whole surface of the furrow once every couple of weeks.

**Harvesting** Harvest eggplants as they mature. You can harvest until the frost hits.

### TIP

Clear up eggplant and mix soil from late October to early November. If onion is planted in late November, you can have a continuous cycle of plant rotation.

## Let's look at the effects

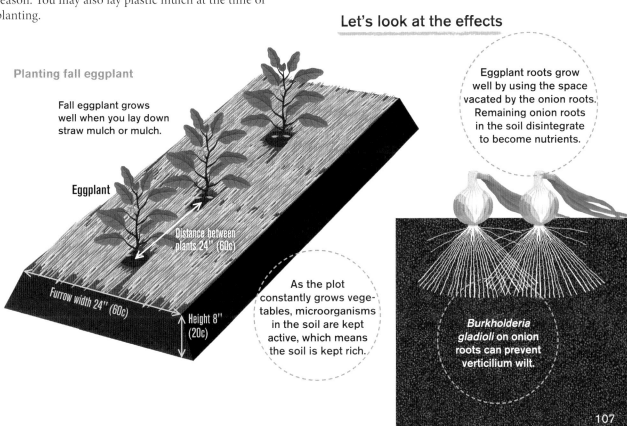

**Planting fall eggplant**

Fall eggplant grows well when you lay down straw mulch or mulch.

Eggplant

Distance between plants 24" (60c)

Furrow width 24" (60c)

Height 8" (20c)

Eggplant roots grow well by using the space vacated by the onion roots. Remaining onion roots in the soil disintegrate to become nutrients.

As the plot constantly grows vegetables, microorganisms in the soil are kept active, which means the soil is kept rich.

*Burkholderia gladioli* on onion roots can prevent verticilium wilt.

107

Speeds up growth

# Burdock (Gobo) & Japanese Leek

## Grow two vegetables with long cultivation periods in order

In Japan, the volcanic ash soil on the Shirasu plateau has good water drainage, which is suited to growing greater burdock (gobo). In contrast, Japanese leek likes sandy soil. While it's ideal to grow Japanese leek on sandy soil, the greater burdock deeply tills the soil with its roots, and that helps Japanese leek grow healthily.

Commonly, you plant greater burdock seeds in fall and harvest it in March to July in the next year. After the harvest, you can plant Japanese leek in mid-to-late September. After harvesting Japanese leek in mid-June of the following year, you can grow greater burdock again. Although greater burdock is known to suffer from repeated cultivation damage, if you use this method you can easily grow two types of plant in a two-year cycle. And neither of these plants requires added fertilizer.

### CULTIVATION PROCESS

**Selecting varieties** Since burdock will be planted in fall, choose varieties which are hard to get bushy in spring. You can choose any type of Japanese leek.

**Making soil** Dig up 24–27½" (60–70 cm) deep three weeks before planting greater burdock to soften the soil. Put the soil back and set up a furrow. Do not apply mature compost or fermented organic fertilizer. You may apply compost when making soil.

**Growing burdock** See p. 57. Sow in mid-late September. Soak the seeds in water for a day before planting. Plant 5–6 seeds in one spot and cover with soil. Thin the plant down to two plants per spot at one leaf and one plant per spot at three leaves.

**Planting Japanese leek** Plant seeds in mid-late September. Planting three seeds per hole will allow the plant to grow well and increase the size of harvest.

**Addition, earthing up** When Japanese leek has grown several leaves, apply fermented organic fertilizer or rice bran on one side of the furrow. After two more weeks, add fertilizer on the other side.

**Harvest** Japanese leek is harvested in late June. Burdock root is harvested if the stem and leaves are dead in June and July.

### TIP

The short variety of greater burdock (salad burdock) can be harvested by the end of September. Another way to pair these plants is to plant salad burdock in the spring of the following year and transition to Japanese leek in the fall.

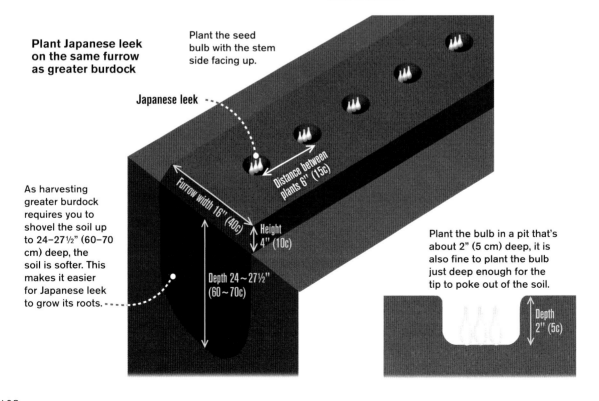

**Plant Japanese leek on the same furrow as greater burdock**

Plant the seed bulb with the stem side facing up.

Japanese leek

Furrow width 16" (40c)

Distance between plants 6" (15c)

Height 4" (10c)

Depth 24~27½" (60~70c)

As harvesting greater burdock requires you to shovel the soil up to 24–27½" (60–70 cm) deep, the soil is softer. This makes it easier for Japanese leek to grow its roots.

Plant the bulb in a pit that's about 2" (5 cm) deep, it is also fine to plant the bulb just deep enough for the tip to poke out of the soil.

Depth 2" (5c)

# Wintering Spinach & Broccoli

## Grow broccoli using the remaining fertilizer in the soil

Did you know that you can also plant spinach in the latter half of fall and it can survive the winter? If you grow spinach seeds in the first half of October, you can harvest spinach in January to February of the following year without having to put much effort into keeping it warm. You can also plant the seeds in November to December if you lay plastic covering over the furrow to harvest spinach in winter. This cultivation method calls for a lot of fertilizer to compensate for low microorganism activity in the soil due to the cold. As a result, there will be a lot of remaining fertilizer in the soil after harvesting the spinach.

Therefore, when you plant broccoli in spring, you won't have to fertilize the soil. You can cultivate broccoli after mixing the dead spinach leaves and roots and making a furrow. Broccoli grows well with the fertilizer that's already in the soil.

### CULTIVATION PROCESS

**Selecting varieties** Spring varieties for spinach are easier to grow. For broccoli, it is good to choose a spring-summer-friendly variety.

**Cultivating spinach** Three weeks before planting, add mature compost and fermented organic fertilizer to prepare. If the soil is acidic, add lime to neutralize. Plant seeds from November to December. Put a vinyl tunnel over the spinach in the middle of December. Grow spinach every 1–1½" (3–4 cm) when it has one leaf, and 2½–3" (6–8 cm) when the plant is 2–2½" (5–6 cm) tall. Fermented organic fertilizer is added in early February.

**Harvesting** Harvest once the plant height is about 10" (25 cm). It is delicious when harvested during the cold season until mid February. It becomes easier to grow bushy in spring.

**Mixing soil at relay time** Do not apply compost or fertilizer, plow lightly to prepare a furrow. The spinach residue can be mixed with the soil.

**Planting broccoli** Seeds are planted in a plastic pot from mid-February to the beginning of March to grow seedlings. Plant seedlings when they have 5–6 leaves, in the end of March to the beginning of April.

**Adding fertilizer, earthing up** Three weeks after planting, add fermented organic fertilizer on one side of the furrow. After another three weeks, add fertilizer to the other side and earth up. Add fertilizer if necessary according to the growth, and if it is not necessary, just earth up.

**Broccoli harvest** Spring-planted broccoli can be harvested 60 to 70 days after planting.

### TIP

Besides broccoli, this method can be applied to radish, burdock, etc., which grow well with relatively little fertilizer. As spinach residue may contaminate the skin of the roots, do not leave the leaves or stems behind.

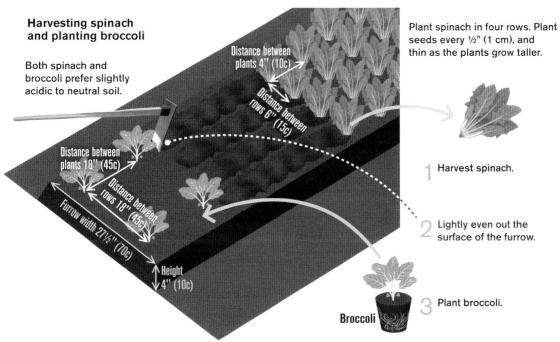

**Harvesting spinach and planting broccoli**

Both spinach and broccoli prefer slightly acidic to neutral soil.

Distance between plants 4" (10c)

Distance between rows 6" (15c)

Distance between plants 18" (45c)

Distance between rows 18" (45c)

Furrow width 27½" (70c)

Height 4" (10c)

Plant spinach in four rows. Plant seeds every ½" (1 cm), and thin as the plants grow taller.

1 Harvest spinach.

2 Lightly even out the surface of the furrow.

3 Plant broccoli.

Broccoli

# Wintering Broccoli & Edamame

Speeds up growth

## Edamame can grow well without the help of residual fertilizers

Wintering broccoli is often cultivated in central to southern area of Japan, where there is little snowfall. For this pairing, plant broccoli seeds in late September to early October, plant the seedlings by late November so that its roots are active by the time temperatures really drop. Once it starts to get warm after February, broccoli will suddenly grow large. You will be able to harvest the broccoli around late March to mid-April.

As broccoli requires little to no fertilizer, there will also be little to no remaining fertilizer after harvesting. Therefore, you should do a lot soil mixing before cultivating another plant, or grow something like edamame which does not require much if any fertilizer. As edamame has root nodule bacteria that captures nitrogen in the atmosphere to turn into nutrients, it can not only feed itself, but can also enrich the soil nearby.

**Application** You can also grow green beans, black-eyed peas, or spring-planted peas instead of edamame.

### CULTIVATION PROCESS

**Selecting varieties** It is easy to grow fall-planted and spring-harvested varieties of broccoli. Use early to middle varieties of edamame.

**Broccoli cultivation** Three weeks before planting, add mature compost and fermented organic fertilizer and prepare a furrow. Plant seeds in plastic pots from late September to early October and grow seedlings. Plant the seedlings with 5–6 leaves by late November.

**Adding fertilizer** Add a fermented organic fertilizer to one side of the furrow in late February and earth up. After another three weeks, add fertilizer to the other side and earth up.

**Harvesting** Harvest when the flower buds grow in late March to mid April. Later, side flower buds can also be harvested.

**Mixing soil at relay** Remove broccoli and tidy up. You do not need to retill the soil extensively, just enough to even out the furrows. Do not add compost or fertilizer.

**Growing edamame** After broccoli has been cleaned up, it can be planted immediately. Prepare seedlings in advance. Sow 2–3 seeds in a plastic pot and grow two per pot at 1½ leaves. Plant the seedling when it has three leaves.

**Additional fertilization** After three weeks from planting, apply fertilizer and earth up. If growth is going as expected, no additional fertilizers are required.

**Harvest** Harvesting should be done if the peapods are plump. Since the cultivation days are determined per the variety, harvest accordingly.

### TIP

This method can be applied to broccoli planted in early summer. The seedlings are grown while being kept warm in January and February. Plant seedlings in March, and harvest in May and June. In this case, plant late varieties sown in July for edamame.

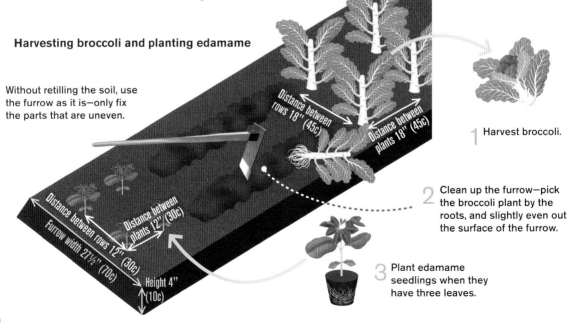

**Harvesting broccoli and planting edamame**

Without retilling the soil, use the furrow as it is—only fix the parts that are uneven.

Distance between rows 18" (45c)

Distance between plants 18" (45c)

Distance between rows 12" (30c)

Distance between plants 12" (30c)

Furrow width 27½" (70c)

Height 4" (10c)

1 Harvest broccoli.

2 Clean up the furrow—pick the broccoli plant by the roots, and slightly even out the surface of the furrow.

3 Plant edamame seedlings when they have three leaves.

# Wintering Broccoli & Fall Potatoes

Speeds up growth

## Disinfect the soil and prevent scab from affecting potatoes, by using the residue

This is a method that takes advantage of a plant type that requires little fertilizer after harvesting broccoli in spring. What is different from the cultivation of edamame on p. 110 is that you can till the remaining leaves, roots and stems into the soil for this method.

Broccoli residue has glucosinolate, a spicy chemical compound unique to Brassicaceae plants, which gets broken down to isothiocyanate. Isothiocyanate has bactericidal effects and can disinfect the soil. If you plant potatoes after harvesting broccoli, you can minimize the possibility of diseases such as scabbing on the potatoes.

## CULTIVATION PROCESS

**Selecting varieties** For broccoli, see p. 110. It is easy to use varieties such as "Dejima," and "Andean red" with short dormancy periods for fall potatoes.

**Broccoli cultivation** See p. 110.

**Mixing soil at relay** When the broccoli harvest is over, cut leaves and stems to a length of about 8" (20 cm), and mix into the soil with the roots. After three or so weeks the soil will be ready.

**Cultivating potatoes** Red potatoes will be planted in early September. See p. 83.

**Harvest**ing When the part above the ground begins to wither after frost hits from late November to early December, dig up the potatoes and harvest.

## TIP

Tilling broccoli residue is basically the same as "soil fumigation" or sterilization and using pesticides. It is also called "biological soil fumigation." It can be widely applied to the Solanaceae and Cucurbitaceae families, in which soil-borne diseases occur frequently. When soil-borne diseases are a frequent problem, it is recommended to also use Chinese mustard, Japanese mustard spinach, or yellow mustard, etc., which contain large amounts of glucosinolate. After mixing the residue into the soil, cover the entire furrow with a clear plastic sheet and seal it for 2–3 weeks for better effect.

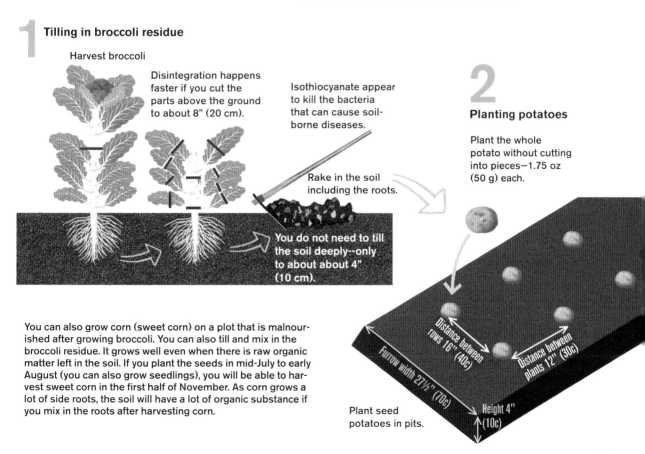

**1 Tilling in broccoli residue**

Harvest broccoli

Disintegration happens faster if you cut the parts above the ground to about 8" (20 cm).

Isothiocyanate appear to kill the bacteria that can cause soil-borne diseases.

Rake in the soil including the roots.

You do not need to till the soil deeply--only to about about 4" (10 cm).

**2 Planting potatoes**

Plant the whole potato without cutting into pieces—1.75 oz (50 g) each.

Distance between rows 16" (40c)

Distance between plants 12" (30c)

Furrow width 27½" (70c)

Height 4" (10c)

Plant seed potatoes in pits.

You can also grow corn (sweet corn) on a plot that is malnourished after growing broccoli. You can also till and mix in the broccoli residue. It grows well even when there is raw organic matter left in the soil. If you plant the seeds in mid-July to early August (you can also grow seedlings), you will be able to harvest sweet corn in the first half of November. As corn grows a lot of side roots, the soil will have a lot of organic substance if you mix in the roots after harvesting corn.

# Combine Mixed Planting & Relay Planting—Annual Plan to Harvest Crops Continuously

When you combine plants well, you can not only use the space efficiently by using companion planting and intercropping methods, but you also use time efficiently by practicing relay planting. This allows you to grow more plant types throughout the year. Here we will raise two examples of an annual plan. You can repeat the same plan next year without worrying about damage from repeated cultivation.

## ● Plan A

### Cultivate a typical plant starting in spring. Grow vegetables properly without much added fertilizer.

After growing and harvesting potatoes, grow typically grown plants such as edamame and corn (sweetcorn) in summer, then plant leafy vegetables such as broccoli and spinach, or root vegetables like daikon and carrots. The feature here is that most of these plants can grow well without much added fertilizer. This allows you to shorten the soil mixing process and use time more efficiently.

### Tips on relay planting

After harvesting potatoes, plant seeds and stand your trellis. Edamame and corn can grow on poor soil without much added soil. Mixed planting of green beans can also enrich the soil.

In fall, add mature compost and fermented organic fertilizer before growing broccoli and spinach as they tend to require more fertilizer. You do not have to add fertilizer if you are growing daikon or carrots after edamame (see p. 76–77).

### Tips on companion planting

Use edamame and corn to speed up growth and to repel pests (see p. 42). Corn and green beans can also speed up growth and repel pests (see p. 38).

Combining broccoli with green leaf lettuce can repel pests (see p. 48). A daikon and green leaf lettuce combination is useful for repelling pests and speeding up growth (see p. 76).

---

**Late March –> Mid-June**

Cultivating potato

Late March: Plant seed potatoes.
Mid-June: Harvest.

**Potato**
It is recommended that you plant the seed potato "upside down" (see p. 82). Harvest in mid-June.

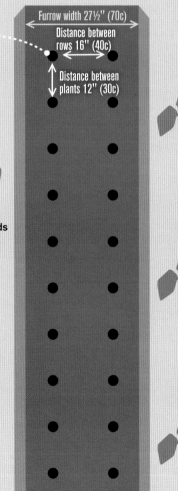

Furrow width 27½" (70c)

Distance between rows 16" (40c)

Distance between plants 12" (30c)

You can prevent diseases if you let weeds like goosefoot and lambsquarters grow.

Earth up the potatoes at 8" (20 cm) in plant height. Earth up again after two more weeks.

## No need to spend time or energy on soil mixing

Potatoes do not require compost or fertilizer if the vegetables have already grown in the space. Prepare a furrow three weeks before planting seed potatoes. If fertilization is properly performed, it is not necessary to retill soil or use much fertilizer when switching between mid-June and late-September.

## Quality will improve if cultivation is repeated

Cultivating vegetables grown with less fertilizer throughout the year stabilizes the soil's condition and reduces pests and diseases. If the same crop is continuously produced each year, it will be easier for the vegetables to grow, and the quality the crop improves.

### Mid-July –> Mid-September
Cultivating edamame and corn

Mid-July: Plant edamame and corn seeds (plus vine type green beans as mixed plant).
Mid-September: Harvest both plants.

### Late September –> early March
Cultivating broccoli, spinach, daikon, and carrot

Late September: Plant broccoli (and green leaf lettuce as a companion). Plant daikon, carrots and spinach as seeds.

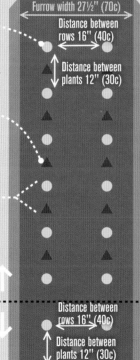

**Corn**
Plant three seeds per spot. Thin the plant with 2–3 leaves to grow one plant per spot. You can also do mixed-planting if you plant green beans.

**Vine type green beans**
The root nodule bacteria on the roots enriches the soil. Can be harvested from mid-August to late September.

As they are from different plant families, they will not be competing against each other.

Grow while adding fermented organic fertilizer.

Do not add any fertilizer from the start up.

**Corn**

**Edamame**
The root nodule bacteria on the roots enriches the soil. Helps corn with growth.

*(furrow labels)* Furrow width 27½" (70c)
Distance between rows 16" (40c)
Distance between plants 12" (30c)
Distance between rows 16" (40c)
Distance between plants 12" (30c)

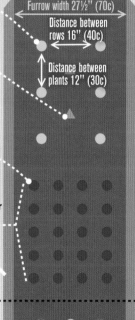

**Broccoli**
Earth up broccoli x2, every three weeks. Harvest in late December to early March.

**Green leaf lettuce**
Plant in rows, and harvest in late October. As the plants come from different plant families, they will not be competing.

**Spinach**
Thin crop x2 by the time it is 2–2½" (5–6 cm) tall. Eventually, distance between plants should be 2½–3" (6–8 cm). Harvest in mid-December to early March.
Distance between rows: 6" (15 cm). Plant seeds every ½" (1 cm).
Add mature compost or fermented organic fertilizer when preparing a furrow.

Do not add any fertilizer from the start.

**Daikon**
Plant 5–7 seeds per spot. Distance between plants is 12" (30 cm). Plant one daikon per spot by thinning x2. Harvest from early December.

**Carrot**
Plant seeds in a line. Thin 2x to space plants at 4–5" (10–12 cm). Harvest from late December to early March.

*(furrow labels)* Furrow width 27½" (70c)
Distance between rows 16" (40c)
Distance between plants 12" (30c)

Being from different families, each repels the other's insects.

# ● Plan B

**Continuous cropping of fruit-type vegetables and other vegetables is possible.**

## Harvest typical vegetables each year while preventing disease.

This is a plan to cultivate in fall, create soil resistant to pests and diseases, and make a good transition from summer to fall fruits and vegetables.

In the first year's fall, leafy vegetables are grown mainly from Brassicaceae plants. From winter to spring, wintering vegetables such as onions, fava beans and peas are grown. From summer to fall, you can grow fruit-type vegetables such as tomatoes, eggplants, peppers, pumpkins and cucumbers. The start of harvest is slower than the general planting timing, which is in early May, so the harvest period is also delayed. However, that results in vegetables that survive the summer healthily and can be harvested until late fall.

### Tips on relay planting

• If soil preparation is carried out before leafy vegetables are cultivated, soil preparation for onion, fava bean and pea can be omitted. In addition, after onion is harvested, there is residual manure, and fava beans and peas make the soil fertile, so it is possible to shift to summer vegetables with minimum effort.
• Antibiotics produced by microorganisms that coexist in the onion root reduce antagonistic bacteria that cause soil-borne diseases in the Cucurbitaceae and Solanaceae families, enabling continuous cropping (see p. 106 and 107).

### Tips on companion planting

Mixed planting of leafy vegetables is effective for evading pests (see p. 60), Chinese cabbage and oats are effective for preventing disease-causing pests (see p. 52), radish and arugula are effective for repelling pests (see p. 72).
• Onions and fava beans/peas combination is effective for promoting growth and preventing pests (see p. 64)
• Solanaceae family and leek, Cucurbitaceae family and scallions are effective for disease prevention (see p. 15, 21, 23, 26 and 30), tomato and basil, eggplant and parsley are effective for repelling pests and speeding up growth (p. 14) 20). Tomato and peanuts are effective for speeding up growth (see p. 12).

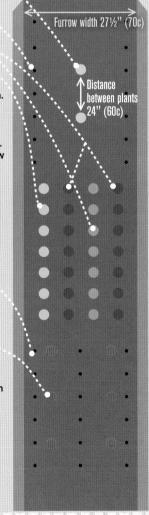

**Mid-September –> early December**

Cultivating leafy vegetables, root vegetables (eg. Chinese cabbage, daikon, potherb mustard, green pak choi, spinach, etc.)

Early September: Plant leafy vegetables, daikon, etc. from seeds. Plant Chinese cabbage seedlings.
Early November to early December: Harvest.

**Chinese cabbage**
Plant as seedlings. Add mature compost and fermented organic fertilizer once in mid-October and once early November.

**Oat**
Planting oat will prevent damage from disease-causing insects.

**Spinach, potherb mustard, green pak choi**
Plant each in rows, 6" (15 cm) between each. Plant seeds every ½" (1 cm). Thin the crop x2 to grow plants every 2½–3" (6–8 cm). Harvest as plants grow bigger, around early November. Planting vegetables from different families can fight pest problems.

**Arugula**
Helps repel pests attracted to daikon. Can be harvested 40 days after planting, while thinning and cropping the plants.

**Daikon**
Plant 5–7 seeds per spot, 16" (40 cm) between rows, one sprout per spot by thinning x2. Harvest in early December.

**Mixing soil**
Three weeks before planting seeds in early September, add mature compost and fermented organic fertilizer to prepare a furrow.

Furrow width 27½" (70c)

Distance between plants 24" (60c)

## If you want to rotate, go to Plan A

After the harvest of onions etc. is over in mid-June, you may move to cultivation Plan A and cultivate green beans and corn. In that case, plan A is a low-nutrition-type plan, so there is no need to prepare soil or add fertilizer.

## If you want plants to work together, plant after mixing the soil

Apply mature compost and base fertilizer in early November, till the soil well, set a furrow up and leave it for about three weeks. Return to cultivating onions, fava beans and peas. If you want to do continuous cropping (wintering vegetables and fruit-type vegetables), you only have to mix soil once each year, in fall.

### Early December –> Mid-June

Cultivating wintering plants
(Onion, fava beans, pea)

Early December: Plant onion, fava beans and pea immediately after preparing a furrow.

### Mid-June to late October

Cultivating fruit-type vegetables
(eggplant, tomato, pumpkin and cucumber)

Mid-June: Lightly adjust the furrow and plant eggplant, tomato, pumpkin and cucumber.

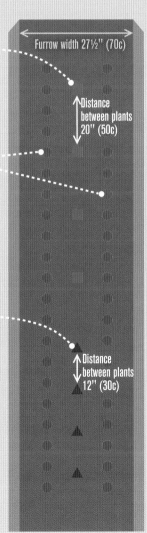

**Fava beans**
Keep 8" (20 cm) away from the onion row. As the root nodule bacteria enriches the soil, do not add fertilizer. Harvest the plant in early May to early June. Also becomes a habitat for beneficial insects.

**Onion**
Plant onions with 4–6" (10–15 cm) in-between. Antibiotic substance in the mycorrhizal bacteria can prevent diseases. Add fertilizer in late December and again in late February. Harvest the plant in mid-June.

**Pea**
Plant pea and keep 8" (20 cm) between pea and onion plants. Root nodule bacteria functions to enrich the soil. Harvest in late April to mid-June.

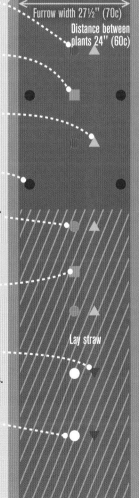

**Tomato**
You do not have to add fertilizer for tomato. Harvest from late July to late October.

**Basil**
Plant basil between tomato plants. It can repel pests and speed up the growth of tomato.

**Garlic chives**
Plant on the foot of tomato, eggplant, green pepper. Prevents diseases.

**Peanuts**
Plant on the side of the furrow. Repels pests and speeds up growth.

**Eggplant or green pepper**
Add fermented organic fertilizer every couple weeks. You can continue harvesting until mid-November.

**Parsley**
Plant parsley between eggplant and green pepper. Repels pests and speeds up growth.

**Scallion**
Plant near the roots of pumpkin and cucumber plants. Prevents diseases.

**Pumpkin or creeping cucumber**
Additional fertilization not necessary. You can harvest the plant until mid-November.

**Guide to Green Manure Cultivation that Enriches the Soil and Makes the Next Run of Crops Grow Better**

# Growing a Green Manure Crop Keeps the Plot Active after Harvesting Vegetables

This keeps the soil's temperature and humidity within a certain range, prevents soil erosion due to rain and wind, and is effective at controlling weeds.

## ● Use the type of green manure that suits your purpose

There are many Gramineae and Fabaceae plants among green manure crops, and they are used depending on the application. All Gramineae grasses grow vigorously, and during the growing season they are used as cleaning crops to collect excess fertilizer in the soil. Not only the stems and leaves above the ground, but also the roots can be used by cutting into the soil. This feeds the soil with organic matter, which will help with soil mixing. The Fabaceae weed family fertilizes the soil through root nodule bacteria symbiosis with the roots during growth. When it is cut and plowed in, it provides a generous amount of nitrogen from leaves and stems.

In addition, there are green manure plants that are used as decoys to control nematode (p. 72), and others, such as yellow mustard pepper (p. 111), that are used for controlling soil pathogens. Flowers such as angelia and sunflower are beautiful and can be used as landscape green fertilizer.

## ● Main green manure crop

### Gramineae green manure crop

**Spring-planted**

Sorgo, Corn, Guinea Grass, Oats, Mulch Wheat, etc.

**Autumn-planted**

Oat, Rye, Italian ryegrass, etc.

### Fabaceae green manure crop

**Spring-to-summer-planted**

Crotalaria, Sesbania, Ebisu grass, etc.

**Fall-planted**

Crimson clover, red clover, hairy vetch, lotus root, etc.

### Other green manure crops

Chinese mustard, marigold, cosmos, sunflower, angelia, barn, buckwheat, etc.

**Sorgo**
Gramineae. Plant height is app. 3–6 feet (1–2 m). Removes excess fertilizer. The roots are plentiful, and they soften the soil. Sorgo is also useful for controlling clubroot disease.

**Oat**
Gramineae. The plant height is 1.5–4.5 feet (0.5–1.5 m). Roots are plentiful and soften the soil. Helps to control clubroot disease.

**Crotalaria**
Fabaceae. Also known as rattlebox. The plant 3–4.5 feet (1–1.5 m) tall. It helps improve soil for deep root types. The soil becomes fertile due to the action of root nodule bacteria. Mix into the soil before the flower blooms. Helps control meadow nematode.

**Crimson clover**
Fabaceae. Plant height is about 1.5 feet (0.5 m). It blooms bright red flowers in spring and can be used as landscape green manure. Soil becomes fertile due to the action of root nodule bacteria symbiosis with roots.

**Hairy vetch**
Fabaceae. Plant height is about 20" (0.5 m) and creeps on the ground. The vine is entwined to form a carpet-like weed. The soil becomes fertile due to the action of root nodule bacteria. Cyanamide released from this plant suppresses weed development.

# Grow Delicious Fruit: Companion Plants for Fruits

## Fruit Cultivation

Just as with vegetables, there are fruit trees that grow better when planted with another type of plant. Here we will introduce some of examples of companion plants for fruit trees. This method also works for trees that have been mature for years.

# Citrus, Rat's-tail Fescue & Hairy Vetch

Speeds up growth   Repels pests   Prevents disease

## Thick cover on the stump hydrates the soil and prevents weeds

Rat's-tail fescue is an annual weed that grows from winter to spring and prevents dehydration of the ground surface. Once it reaches a height of about 20" (50 cm), ears start to form and the plant starts to die. If you shear the plant to a height of about 4–6" (10–15 cm), you can forestall the emergence of the ears and maintain the green stems. In this way, the rat's-tail fescue prevents other weeds from growing in the summer, and becomes a type of raw fertilizers in fall. This not only protects and hydrates the root, but allows the plant to become a habitat for beneficial insects that kill pests that invade fruit trees.

Hairy vetch can be used in a similar way. As it has strong allelopathy, it eliminates other types of weeds. By June it will die and become carpet-like on the ground. As it is an Alliaceae plant, its root nodule bacteria can enrich the soil as well.

**Application** You can also use this method on plum, peach, Japanese pear or blueberries. You can also use Italian ryegrass, crimson clover or red clover instead of the weeds outlined above.

### CULTIVATION PROCESS

**Selecting varieties** Any species of citrus will work. Rat's-tail fescue and hairy vetch seeds are sold as green manure.

**Mixing soil** Choose a well-drained, sunny place. Cover the area to be planted with mulch about a month prior to planting.

**Planting citrus** Spring is the right time. Complete planting by the beginning of April.

**Rat's-tail fescue, hairy vetch seeding** Sprinkle seeds under citrus trees at the end of September to early October and lightly cover with soil.

**Adding fertilizer** For citrus, add fertilizer such as dregs once in June and in March, and add fermented organic fertilizer in June and October. If planting with rat's-tail fescue apply approximately 30% more fertilizer to citrus. In the case of hairy vetch, use less fertilizer.

**Harvesting** Citrus fruits are harvested at appropriate times. To extract seeds from rat's-tail fescue, harvest the dead ears in July, dry them, and extract the seeds in September. You can harvest hairy vetch seeds from the bush around July.

**Citrus Tailing** The second year after planting, cut back to 20–24" (50–60 cm) tall, and at the same time, cut back the part that grew in the previous fall. In the third year, the part that had grown in the previous summer is cut back in spring and branches in the crowded section are thinned out

### TIP

You may leave rat's-tail fescue without cutting it. It will wither in July and, become a carpet that suppresses summer weeds. Although spilled seeds germinate in the fall, their growth may be uneven, so it's better to harvest some seeds and replant. The same goes for hairy vetch. Be careful to manage their prevalence in the garden, as both tend to become invasive.

Example of tangerine farmers using rat's-tail fescue. As many citrus farms have slopes, weeds can help prevent soil erosion.

**Planting rat's-tail fescue and hairy vetch seeds**

Same process even when citrus trees are already planted.

Plant the seeds around late September to early October. Lightly cover the seeds with soil. You can plant the seeds at the same time that you add fertilizer.

# Grape & Chinese Plantain

Prevents disease

## Prevent mildew by increasing mycoparasites with the use of Chinese plantain

The grape plant is native to dry-summer climates. If you are trying to grow grapes in a hot, humid climate, you could encounter mildew, a white, powdery mold that prevents photosynthesis and slows down the growth of the vine. Mold will also affect the fruits, inhibiting maturation.

Chinese plantain is a plant that, while also affected by mildew, has a different type of bacteria. The mycoparasite that attaches to the mildew on the plantain can positively affect the grape vine by killing the mildew on the vine.

**Application** This method is also effective on apple trees, which also often sustain damage from mildew. You can also apply this to fruits such as strawberry, cucumber, pumpkin, watermelon, or tomatoes.

### CULTIVATION PROCESS

**Selecting varieties** Any variety will work for grapes but generally, American grape varieties are more disease-resistant than European grapes.

**Cultivating grapes** Choose a well-drained area with good sun exposure, lay down mulch around November to March, and then plant grape saplings on a slightly higher spot. After planting, cut the main branch to about 20" (50 cm) to promote side branch extension.

**Management of plantains** If it grows naturally, leave it as it is. Around early to late summer, spikes will grow and develop seeds. It is good to collect them before they spill, and plant them in the fall beneath the grape stock.

**Tailing grapes, pruning** Spread the extended branches over the arbor. Select several side branches and arrange over the arbor as well. In winter of the second year, cut back the main branch. Shoots that developed before going dormant will gradually grow new shoots. After the third year, cut branches that grew in the previous year at 5–8th node. A bunch of fruit will grow on branches that have grown from these shoots.

**Setting aside, thinning, putting on a bag** When flowering begins in May, cut the flower bunch to adjust its shape and limit its size. In June, nip the flower buds so that there will be one fruit bunch per branch. You may want to bag the fruit as soon as the bunch is full.

**Fertilizing** Apply organic fertilizer, composed mainly of dregs, as cold fertilizer in February. Supplement with fermented organic fertilizer in June and September.

**Harvesting** Harvest when the grapes are mature and in full color.

### TIP

There is a way to spread the seeds of barley and oats on one side to make a cover crop (green manure) in places where Chinese plantains do not grow well. Both barley and oat are susceptible to powdery mildew, and will attract mycoparasites that can kill the mildew bacteria. If you plant the seeds in spring, you can maintain a low plant height without producing spikes. The plants wither in fall and supply organic matter.

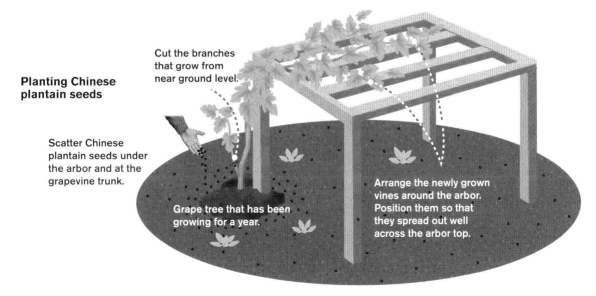

**Planting Chinese plantain seeds**

Cut the branches that grow from near ground level.

Scatter Chinese plantain seeds under the arbor and at the grapevine trunk.

Grape tree that has been growing for a year.

Arrange the newly grown vines around the arbor. Position them so that they spread out well across the arbor top.

# Blueberry & Mint

Repels pests    Speeds up growth

## While hydrating the soil, repel pests using the scent of herb

Blueberry grows shallow roots and likes acidic soil. This makes it harder for other types of plants to grow near the foot of blueberry plants. On the other hand, mint spreads its root in a wide area and dominates the plot. Yet, when these two plants are cultivated together, their partnership somehow works well, and the mint can aid the blueberry plants' growth.

One explanation for this is that mint can keep the soil moist to allow blueberry to grow long branches and flower buds. In addition, the unique scent of mint repels pests that are attracted to blueberry.
**Application** Mint also works well with other berry plants such as blackberry. You can also grow thyme instead of mint.

### CULTIVATION PROCESS

**Selecting varieties** The varieties of blueberries include northern highbushes that are suitable for cold regions, southern highbushes that are suitable for warm regions, and rabbiteye types. It is good to grow two or more different varieties to make pollination easier. You can use general standing mint or creeping mint bushes.

**Soil preparation** As blueberry prefers acid soil, mix unadjusted acidity peat moss into the soil where you will be planting.

**Planting** Blueberries should be planted in November and March. Take care to avoid planting too deeply. Plant mint from late March, 12" (30 cm) away from the foot of the blueberry.

**Adding fertilizer** Fertilize blueberries in March and after harvesting the berries. Not necessary for mint.

**Harvesting** Blueberries are harvested as they mature. Mint can be picked as it grows.

**Tailing blueberries** Cut back the tip of the branch so as to prevent excessive flower buds in March, or thin the resulting branch. The old branches with poor production are thinned in winter, and grow the side shoots that stem from the old branch.

### TIP

Mint should always be pruned to a height of about 6" (15 cm). Use the cut leaves. By cutting/picking frequently, the smell is stronger, enhancing its pest control effects. In addition, if pruning is done so that the flowers do not bloom, it can be harvested until the frost hits.

Mint stays close by the blueberry bush. Other acidic soil, aromatic herbs such as basil and thyme are good companions for blueberries.

**Planting mint**

Plant mint in a circle surrounding blueberry. Leave about 12" (30 cm) distance from the blueberry.

Choose a place that gets plenty of sunlight and good water drainage.

Add peat moss and mix with soil near where blueberry is going to be planted.

Plant mint in the same way even if blueberry is already growing on the plot.

12" (30c)

# Currants & Vetch

## Induce the growth of currants by hydrating the soil near the base

There are different types of currants—redcurrant, whitecurrant, and blackcurrant which is also known as cassis. They are native to Europe, so they do well against the cold winter, and poorly where summers are hot. Basically, the cultivation of currants is suitable for areas with colder climates.

The mixed cultivation of currants and common vetch has been observed in the Americas for some time. You can use a winter vetch to serve as a cover crop. Vetch starts growing around March and spreads its vines like a carpet on the ground. Throughout winter and spring, this can keep the ground moist and induce the sprouting of currants, and also aids the growth of the currants afterwards. As a result, currants will have plentiful flowers and bear good quality fruits. As vetch is a Fabaceae plant, the root nodule bacteria can capture nitrogen and enrich the soil. When it dies in summer, it will cover the ground with its dead leaves and vines to keep the soil cool and hydrated. It can also prevent other types of weeds from growing. In the end, it will be broken down into raw organic matter to further enrich the soil.

### CULTIVATION PROCESS

**Selecting varieties** Can be any variety. Vetches are easy to grow in cold regions. Plant late to keep the plant green for longer.

**Cultivating currants** Choose a sunny place. If you opt for a place that's sunny in the morning but shady in the afternoon, your plants won't survive the summer. Lay mulch to prepare the soil. Plant in December to February. Thin out the crowded part of the branch from January to February. Branches will age when harvested for 4 -5 years, so it is better to grow new shoots that sprout from the bottom of the bush.

**Vetch seeding** Sprinkle seeds around the roots of currants in October-November, and lightly cover the soil.

**Adding fertilizer** Currants are fertilized in February, and again in October. Use organic fertilizer composed mainly of dregs. Because vetch helps fertilize the soil, you can use less fertilizer than you would if you grow currants on their own.

**Harvest** The harvest period is from late June to mid-July. Harvest fruit that's mature and in full color.

### TIP

While vetch's allelopathic effect is strong, monitor it carefully as it can become invasive. Still, it is a convenient mulch for fruit trees. It's best to use winter vetch in cold regions and hairy vetch in warm regions.

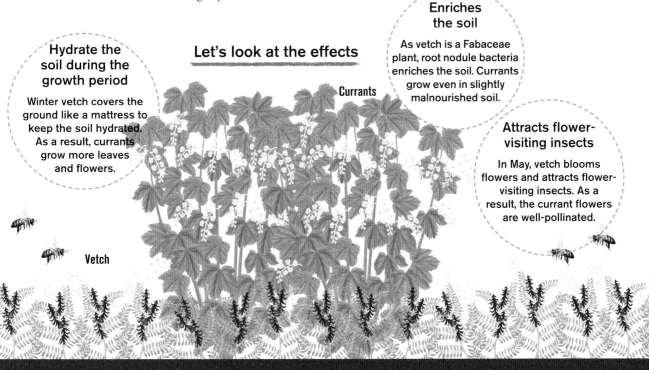

## Let's look at the effects

**Enriches the soil**

As vetch is a Fabaceae plant, root nodule bacteria enriches the soil. Currants grow even in slightly malnourished soil.

**Hydrate the soil during the growth period**

Winter vetch covers the ground like a mattress to keep the soil hydrated. As a result, currants grow more leaves and flowers.

**Attracts flower-visiting insects**

In May, vetch blooms flowers and attracts flower-visiting insects. As a result, the currant flowers are well-pollinated.

Currants

Vetch

# Fig & Loquat

Repels pests

## Reduce pest damage by planting loquat together

Loquats are exotic to many areas, comfortable only in climates that don't dip below freezing. In Japan they are often grown alongside figs. The conventional wisdom is that loquat trees repel longicorn beetles, which are attracted to fig trees.

### CULTIVATION PROCESS

**Selecting varieties** Any variety will work for both plants.

**Cultivating figs** Choose a sunny, well-drained place. Because it prefers neutral soil, mix lime with bitter clay when making soil. Plant in November to March. Cut at a height of 20" (50 cm) and mix cuttings with soil to use as mulch. Leave three side branches in the second winter and prune the others. In the winter after the third year, the shoots that have grown in the previous year should be thinned out or cut back to adjust their shape.

**Cultivating loquat** Choose a sunny, well-drained spot, lay mulch to prepare the soil. Plant from late February to late March. Fix it with a trellis. Prune in September every year as flowers and fruits are grown in winter. The overlapping branches should be thinned out, and the branches that are too long should be cut back at the tip.

Because the growth is vigorous, the tree height will rise very quickly.

**Fertilization** Add cold fertilization in February. Add fertilizer in June and October. Add cold fertilization to loquat in March, and add fertilizer in June and September. Cold fertilizers are organic fertilizer consisting mainly of dregs. Additional fertilizers are fermented organic fertilizer.

**Nipping, pruning** Not necessary for figs. Loquat will be pruned from October. Leave one or more lower tiers in one cluster and drop the upper tiers. Leave a few fruits in lower fruit bunch from late March to early April, and perform bagging. It is recommended that the quantity of leftovers be kept small for large varieties, and bigger for medium-sized varieties.

**Harvesting** The figs' harvest period ranges from late June to late September depending on the variety. Harvest when the fruit is colorful and ripe. Harvest ripe loquat from the middle of May to the end of June.

### TIP

As the longicorn beetles cause enormous damage to citrus fruits such as mandarin orange, it is also effective to pair with loquat. Both grow well in warm climates and the cultivation environment is also compatible.

## Let's look at the effects

**Repels longicorn beetles**

It is effective enough to have loquat trees a little far away from the fig tree. If you are growing many figs, it is enough to plant one loquat tree per ten fig trees.

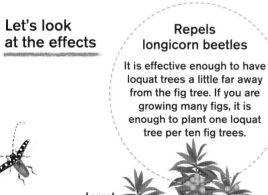

Loquat

As loquat tree sometimes have white root rot, it is recommended that you plant garlic chives near the tree (see p. 124).

Garlic chives

Fig

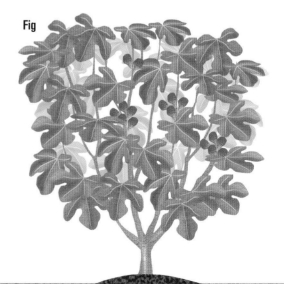

Little damage caused by longicorn beetles.

A lot of damage caused by longicorn beetles.

# Persimmon & Japanese Leek

Speeds up growth

## Reduce premature fruit dropping and grow healthy Japanese leek

In Japan, persimmon has long been a fixture in Japan's home gardens. Near the stump, Japanese leek had always been grown. Their compatibility must have been known for ages.

Persimmon often prematurely drops fruits during late June to mid-September. One reason for this is dehydration during the summer. If you grow Japanese leek near the stump, you can increase the size of harvest, as hydrating the ground can prevent premature dropping. As Japanese leek dislikes strong sunlight and dehydration, it grows well under the persimmon tree.

Japanese leek stems will die and cover the ground with dead leaves and stems in November. This prevents various types of weed from growing in winter. It is also fine to cut the dead leaves and scatter them around. The dead leaves will disintegrate and become nutrients for persimmon during winter.

## CULTIVATION PROCESS

**Selecting varieties** Any variety will work for both plants.

**Cultivating persimmon** Plant in a sunny place between November and March. Commercial grafted trees can be harvested four years after planting.

**Cultivating Japanese leek** Plant in the middle of March. At about 12" (30 cm) away from the persimmon tree trunk, plant leek seed stocks (root stock) in a circle at 16" (40 cm) between stocks. If a persimmon tree has already been planted and is growing, plant the leek further away from the tree trunk.

**Adding fertilizer** Fertilizer is added three times for persimmon: cold fertilization in December/January, additional fertilization in July and October. Additional fertilization is not necessary for leeks.

**Harvest** Persimmon fruits are harvested as they mature.

Leek is harvested as flower leek in fall of the first year, and is harvested in summer in the second year. Dig up the leek if it is visible above ground.

**Tailing persimmon** Trim the persimmon branches so that there is one central branch. Tailoring is done during winter when the leaves have fallen. Prune the main trunk 27½–31½" (70–80 cm) in the first year. In the second year, the top branch is cut to ⅓ and the other side branches are removed. In the third year, cut the top branch in half and leave two lower side branches. After that, cut the branch grown in the second year, and keep the first-year branch as the result branch.

## TIP

After three years, leek becomes fatigued and growth becomes sluggish. Dig up the seed stock and transplant it little by little while considering the spread of the persimmon tree crown.

Japanese leek grows well in shade created by the persimmon tree.

**In case if this is your first year growing persimmon**

Persimmon

Plant tree seedlings with three sprouts at 3–4" (8–10 cm) deep.

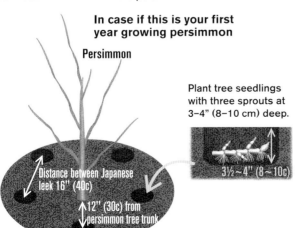

3½ ~ 4" (8 ~ 10c)

Distance between Japanese leek 16" (40c)

↑12" (30c) from persimmon tree trunk

Place in good sunlight.

**If the persimmon tree is already growing**

Plant Japanese leek on the edge of the area around the persimmon tree.

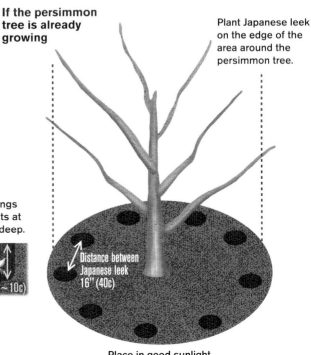

Distance between Japanese leek 16" (40c)

Place in good sunlight.

# Plum & Garlic Chives

Prevents disease

## Surround the area around the tree trunk to prevent diseases

Plum (and prune) often struggle to grow new branches in spring, or may grow damaged leaves on the outside of the tree canopy. Though flower buds will still grow, fruits won't grow well, and the tree's growth will slowly decline. This is due to a disease called white root rot, which is caused by mold bacteria invading the roots of the tree. The bacteria chokes up the fibrovascular bundles, and eventually kills the tree. This is a common disease for Japanese plum, apple and Japanese pear trees.

You can eliminate the bacteria by utilizing the good bacteria living on the garlic chive roots. In Japan, this method has long been practiced by some of the farmers who produce plums.

**Application** This method is also effective with prunus plants such as apricot and Japanese plum.

### CULTIVATION PROCESS

**Selecting varieties** If you would like to harvest fruits, be aware that the tree will usually require another tree for pollination. Any variety can work for garlic chives.

**Plum cultivation** Plant in a sunny, well-drained area. Poor drainage is likely to cause white root rot. Improve the soil by adding mature compost and mulch. Plant it slightly shallow in November to March. Cut the main branch by 20" (50 cm), and leave two main branches in the second winter. Grow the branch diagonally. After the third year, cut back the branches that have grown, and let out short branches.

**Planting garlic chives** Mid-May to mid-June are the best seasons, but can be planted at any time during the year except in winter. Separate from the plum roots and plant around the new roots (tree crown) to surround the trees.

**Adding fertilizer** Add cold fertilization in February, and in May and October for plum. It is not necessary to add fertilizer for garlic chives.

**Harvesting** Depends on the type. Japanese sour plum is harvested from late June to late August, and prune is from late August to late September. Harvest the fruits as they mature. See p. 63 for chive.

### TIP

White root rot also occurs on other fruit trees. There is a traditional Japanese farming method that pairs apples that are mainly grown in cold areas with Japanese chives.

Example of planting garlic chives under the plum tree.

**In case if you are planting a sapling**

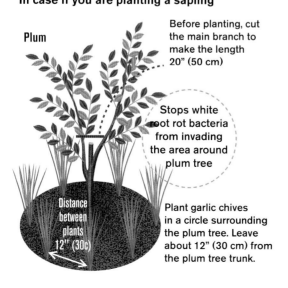

Plum

Before planting, cut the main branch to make the length 20" (50 cm)

Stops white root rot bacteria from invading the area around plum tree

Distance between plants 12" (30c)

Plant garlic chives in a circle surrounding the plum tree. Leave about 12" (30 cm) from the plum tree trunk.

**If the plum tree is already growing**

Changes caused by white root rot can be seen first near the tree crown. Symptoms of white root rot are yellowing buds/leaves, misshapen flowers and so on.

Branches and roots near the tree crown are connected.

Plant garlic chives in a circle surrounding the tree crown of plum tree

Distance between plants 12" (30c)

# Olive & Potatoes, Fava Beans, etc.

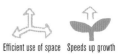

Efficient use of space    Speeds up growth

## Grow vegetables between winter and early summer using the space under the tree

This is a common practice observable in organic olive farms in Mediterranean countries such as Italy and Spain. You can grow vegetables like potatoes, fava beans or onions using the empty space under the olive tree. This diversifies the soil environment, and will reduce pest damage. Also, companion plants will develop a network of mycorrhizal bacteria, which will enhance each other's growth. As olive is an evergreen tree, it can also function as a wind shield for the vegetables.

Other than vegetables, you can also grow common vetch as green manure, as it will hydrate the ground between winter and spring. The root nodule bacteria on the vetch roots will also enrich the soil.

## CULTIVATION PROCESS

**Choosing varieties** Olives require pollination in order to bear fruit, so consider pollination methods when choosing your variety. Some varieties self-pollinate, others pollinate through wind, while still others require a cross-pollinating tree. As for onions, potatoes and fava beans, any variety will do.

**Cultivating olives** Choose a sunny spot with good drainage. Olives prefer neutral soil, so it's good to add some lime to the humus when mixing the soil. After planting, cut to a height of about 20" (50 cm). After the second year, between February and March, prune branches that have grown too long. Thin out branches when and as needed. Pick the fruits between mid-July and mid-August.

**Cultivating potatoes, beans and onions** For potatoes, see p. 80; for fava beans and onions, see p. 64–65.

**Fertilization** Fertilize olives in March, June and November. For other vegetables, follow their respective cultivation times.

**Harvesting** Harvest olives between October and November.

## TIP

If growing olive trees in containers, and combining with onions that don't require a lot of space, consider adding leeks to the mix. Herbs or grasses can also be grown.

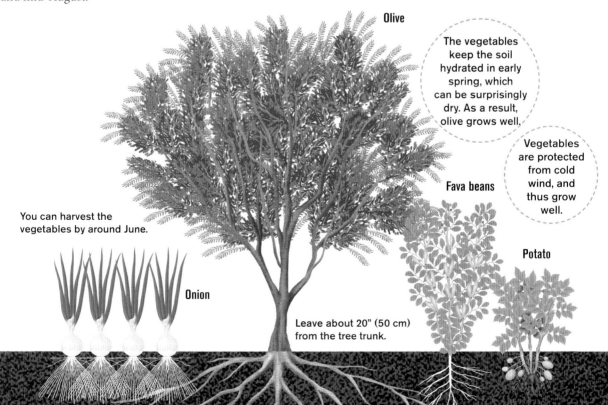

Olive

The vegetables keep the soil hydrated in early spring, which can be surprisingly dry. As a result, olive grows well.

Fava beans

Vegetables are protected from cold wind, and thus grow well.

Potato

You can harvest the vegetables by around June.

Onion

Leave about 20" (50 cm) from the tree trunk.

# Companion Plants Chart
## Good combinations and expected effects

| Plant | Companion plants | Prevents diseases | Repels pests | Speeds up growth | Efficient use of space | Relay planting | Page |
|---|---|---|---|---|---|---|---|
| Bitter melon | Okinawa chickweed | | ● | ● | ● | | – |
| | Green beans (with vines) | | ● | ● | ● | | 47 |
| | Garlic chives | ● | | | | | – |
| Blueberry | Mint | | ● | ● | | | 124 |
| Broccoli | Salvia | | ● | | | | 49, 68 |
| | Lettuce | | ● | | ● | | 48, 62 |
| | Ginger | | | ● | ● | | – |
| | Fava beans | | ● | ● | | | 50 |
| | Chickweed/clover | | | ● | | | 51 |
| | Spinach | | | | | ● | 109 |
| | Edamame | | | ● | | ● | 110 |
| | Red potato | | | ● | | | 111 |
| Cabbage | Red leaf lettuce | | ● | | | | 48 |
| | Carrot | | ● | | | | – |
| | Salvia | | ● | | | | – |
| | Chickweed/clover | | ● | ● | | | 36, 51 |
| | Daikon | ● | | | | ● | 103 |
| Carrot | Edamame | | ● | ● | | ● | 75, 98 |
| | Daikon/radish | | ● | ● | | | 76 |
| | Turnip/green pak choi | | | ● | | | 76 |
| Chinese cabbage | Nasturtium | | ● | | | | 53 |
| | Lettuce | | ● | | | | – |
| | Oat | ● | ● | ● | | | 52, 69 |
| | Edamame | | | ● | | ● | 96 |
| Corn | Soybeans (edamame) | | ● | ● | | | 42, 69 |
| | Adzuki beans | | ● | ● | | | 40 |
| | Green bean (with vines) | | ● | | ● | | 38 |
| | Pumpkin | | | ● | ● | | 28 |
| | Watermelon | | | ● | ● | | 28 |
| | Japanese hornwort | | | ● | | | 41 |
| | Taro | | | | ● | | 41 |
| | Purslane | | | ● | | | – |
| Crown daisy | Brassicaceae vegetables | | ● | | | | 58, 60 |
| | Basil | | ● | | | | 59 |
| Cucumber | Scallions | ● | ● | | | | 26 |
| | Wheat | | ● | | | | 27, 69 |
| | Taro | | | | ● | | 24 |
| | Garlic | ● | | | | ● | 101 |
| Currants | Vetch | | ● | ● | | | 121 |
| Daikon | Chickweed | | ● | ● | | | 72 |
| | Eggplant | | | ● | ● | | 19 |
| | Marigold | | | ● | | | 72 |
| | Taro | | | | ● | | 86 |
| | Sweet potato | | | ● | | | 104 |
| | Carrot | | ● | ● | | | 76 |
| | Arugula | ● | | ● | | | 72 |
| | Turnip | | | ● | | | 77 |
| | Edamame | | | ● | | ● | 98 |
| | Cabbage | ● | | | | ● | 98 |
| Devil's tongue | Oat | ● | | | | | – |
| Edamame | Corn | | ● | ● | | | 42, 69 |

| Plant | Companion plants | Prevents diseases | Repels pests | Speeds up growth | Efficient use of space | Relay planting | Page |
|---|---|---|---|---|---|---|---|
| Edamame | Red leaf lettuce | ● | ● | | | | 44 |
| | Mint | | ● | | | | 45 |
| | Carrot | | | ● | | ● | 75, 98 |
| | Chinese cabbage | | | ● | | | 96 |
| | Daikon | | | ● | | | 98 |
| | Wintering broccoli | | | ● | | | 100 |
| Eggplant | Parsley | | ● | ● | ● | | 20, 69 |
| | Garlic chives | ● | ● | | | | 21 |
| | Peanuts | | | ● | ● | | 12 |
| | Green beans (vineless) | | ● | ● | ● | | 18 |
| | Ginger | | ● | ● | | | 16 |
| | Daikon | | | ● | ● | | 19 |
| | Onion | ● | | | | ● | 107 |
| Fava beans | Olive | | ● | ● | ● | | 125 |
| | Spring cabbage | | ● | ● | ● | | 50, 69 |
| | Onion | ● | | ● | ● | | 64 |
| Fig | Loquat | | ● | | | | 122 |
| Garlic | Crimson clover | | ● | ● | | | – |
| | Strawberry | | ● | ● | | | 88 |
| | Okra | ● | ● | | | ● | 105 |
| | Cucumber | ● | | ● | | | 101 |
| Garlic chives | Goosefoot | | | ● | | | 63 |
| | Plum | ● | | | | | 124 |
| Ginger | Taro | | | ● | ● | | 84 |
| | Eggplant | ● | | ● | ● | | 16 |
| | Broccoli | | | ● | ● | | – |
| Grape | Chinese plantain | ● | | | | | 119 |
| | Wood sorrel | | ● | | | | – |
| Greater burdock | Japanese leek | | | ● | | ● | 108 |
| | Spinach | | | ● | ● | | 57 |
| Green bean | Arugula | | ● | ● | | | 46 |
| | Eggplant | | ● | ● | ● | | 18 |
| | Sweet potato | ● | ● | ● | ● | | 79 |
| | Btter melon | | ● | ● | | | 47 |
| | Corn | | ● | ● | | | 38 |
| Green onion | Spinach | ● | ● | | | | 56, 69 |
| | Turnip | | ● | | | | 70 |
| Green pak choi | Crown daisy | | ● | | | | 58, 60 |
| | Scallions | ● | ● | | | | 60, 70 |
| | Green leaf lettuce | | ● | ● | | | 60, 71 |
| | Carrot | | | ● | | | 76 |
| | Tomato | | | | | ● | 100 |
| Green pepper | Green beans | | ● | | ● | | 18 |
| | Nasturtium | | ● | | | | 22 |
| | Peanuts | | | ● | ● | | 12 |
| | Garlic chives | ● | ● | | | | 23 |
| | Spinach/lettuce | | | ● | ● | ● | 102 |
| Japanese leek | Greater burdock | | | ● | | | 108 |
| Japanese mustard spinach | Goosefoot/Lambsquarters | | | ● | | | 36, 55 |
| | Crown daisy | ● | | | | | 58 |

126